DARE TO UNLOCK
THE DOOR

A Journey to Freedom and Wholeness

By J.W. Pratt

To contact the publisher, visit www.paragonpublishing.co.uk
To contact the author, visit www.JWPratt.org

Library of Congress Cataloging-in-Publication Data is available upon request.

ISBN: 978-1-3999-0284-7

Printed in the United States of America

Cover Artwork by Dane Dewar, entitled, 'Girl in a Dark Room.'
All rights reserved.

Book cover design and layout Paragon Publishing.

First Edition

TABLE OF CONTENTS

DEDICATION PAGE

This book is dedicated to every grown child who has dared to be brave enough to open the hidden door of hurt, pain, shame, and disfunction, and take the difficult journey to wholeness.

To my sister Dawn one of the bravest, strongest, discerning and selfless women I have known. Gone too young, too soon, forever with me.

To the memory of my mother who loved all she could and gave all she had.

My Brother Donovan, I am lost for words at your sudden passing. You found a way to rise to inspire and touch so many. The grief is fresh right now. You will be forever missed.

To my husband Randy, my love and consistent pillar to lean on. You continually cover me, encourage me, and help me to always reach for my dreams.

To our children Randy 3rd, Tally, Tamera (aka Bean), and our miracle boy Carrington, who changed my life and fills my heart.

Most importantly, to God my Savior. I am so in awe of You Lord. You loved me, covered, and carried me through ALL of life's twists and turns, bumps and bruises. I now understand, every hill, valley, and dark place was necessary for my journey, which brought me to that appointed place where You flooded every hidden chamber with Your light and life. You didn't just want me Holy, You cared about bringing me to a place of wholeness.

ACKNOWLEDGMENTS

Professor Paul Staup - You skillfully and gently peaked into my soul and began the process that would unlock the door.

Professor Martin Sanders - Thank you for following Gods' lead, committing to, and taking the time to help me uncover the painful truth of my wounded inner child.

Professor John and Mrs. Ellenberger - You are truly anointed with a powerful ministry. Thank you for standing in the gap and skillfully guiding me to complete freedom and a path to wholeness.

Got to thank my spiritual family and warriors in the faith, June & Robert, Dottie, Fitz & Delores, Virginia & Mike, and Deacon Karen. For your prayers, encouragement and even getting in the trenches with me to war and take back what the enemy wanted to steal.

Dr. Morais Cassell - Thank you for your candid critique and insight. It didn't hurt as bad as I thought it would. Lol.

My Sista from another mother, Beverly (My mate) decades of friendship, adventures, and sisterhood.

Doreen - A spiritual sister and Armor-bearer like no other, thank you for your steadfast covering and ministry.

Bishop B.L.Trogden - You opened the door for me to begin ministering regionally as Director of Children's Ministry and Christian Education.

My spiritual parents both covered and challenged me. You saw something in me God could use. Bishop Rufus and Verona Rogers for covering me and counting me as part of the family. So many happy Thanksgiving memories and heart-to-heart words of wisdom kept me grounded.

Bishop Cervin and Sylvia McKinnon, thank you both for your open hearts, love, and encouragement. You made sure I knew you were in my corner.

Thank you to my sis, Azania, and the team at Paragon Publishing for believing in the message of this story and for giving your time, talent, and expertise to bringing this all to life.

Thank you to Dewar Designs, Dane you are the best, thank you for capturing and bringing the vision in my mind to life with your cover illustration.

To Angelina and all those who encouraged me to tell my story, who prayed and supported this process, thank you for not letting me back down.

Thank you, Taylor, from Jovanovic Photography, for taking the author's picture featured on the back of this book. It was a fun and enjoyable experience, an excellent job.

Thank you to the beauty team who facilitated hair and make-up for my pictures; Hair by Arts of Love salon & Spa, and makeup by O'Linda Forbes at Cano Creations.

This has been a marvelous journey and everyone mentioned has contributed to my life more than you will ever know. Thanking every one from my heart.

To God be all the Glory.

FOREWORD

*G*od wastes nothing. I have learned this truism to be both biblically correct and theologically sound. However, there have been times when its reality, because of what I was experiencing, seemed psychologically and pragmatically unsettling. Yet, this is the redemptive work of the Triune God. Where abuse, generational dysfunction, and injustices abound, the grace of God does much more abound (Romans 5:20)! God does indeed specialize in granting beauty for ashes, He gives the oil of joy in the place of mourning, as He reverses the spirit of heaviness with a garment of praise (Isaiah 61:3). However, while regeneration is immediate, the redemptive work of our transformed lives, growing in grace, is a life-long process.

Janet Waite-Pratt invites the reader to join her as she shares her journey to wholeness. Within these pages, you will read of her conversion to Christ and miraculous physical healing. You will also read of her journey to emotional, familial, and spiritual healing. Perhaps you will come to discern that this is not just Janet's story; it is the untold story of many fellow travelers who, like Janet, are on a similar journey.

As you read the pages of this manuscript, I suspect, you will experience moments of celebration coupled with emotions of disbelief, anger, and even grief as you process the visceral suffering of a fellow traveler, an Imago Dei. There are pages of this book you may find difficult to read. I suspect, they were excruciating to write. Perhaps, the difficulty for some readers will be enhanced because of similar developmental experiences and abuses in one's own life. Memories long-past, repressed, and wished to be forgotten may resurface. Consequently, the reader may discover that he/she will only be able to read and process a few pages at a time. Do not rush the reading. The reader may also find that reading with other trusted confidantes, in a safe place, who are also on a journey to wholeness, to be helpful.

Janet allows the reader into her world to experience her life struggles of self-image issues, doubts of self-worth, and negative self-talk. She allows you to view the unwritten rules characteristic of many dysfunctional family systems: don't ask, don't feel, don't trust, and don't talk. In this type of family dysfunction, secrets are a way of life. However, the author also shares the freedom that comes in the light of releasing every detail of one's life to the sovereign Savior. Her story is not simply about abuse and injustice, which should never occur in one's life; it is also about the healing that forgiveness brings to the wounded soul. Indeed, a decision to forgive is a decision to heal.

Janet's journey to wholeness has not only unlocked the abused little girl with which you will become acquainted. You will also be introduced to a godly, gifted, and gracious woman who has emerged through God's sovereign design. However, it took time. The process did not occur immediately. Today, she has a platform in which to lead worship and share ministry as she encourages fellow travelers to keep progressing on the pathway to wholeness. Her devotion to the heavenly Father is marked.

Her passion for the Savior is without question. The fruit of the Holy Spirit is evident in her life. Consequently, her commitment to wholeness in the lives of others is unwavering. My prayer is that Janet's story will be a source of encouragement to each reader who continues to travel the pathway of wholeness. May you be confident that He who has begun a good work in you will carry it on to completion until the day of Christ (Philippians 1:6).

-Tim Harper, DMin.

Regional Bishop

INTRODUCTION

Only when one has persevered and finally outgrown the box of limitations or, is brought to the brink of breaking, do you begin to discover the remarkable inner strength we all have to rise, despite being challenged. It is the strength to take a leap of faith and not give in to our struggles and our fears. On the brink when you feel as though you are about to be consumed, you must make the choice, do you give up on what hope says is possible and crumble into an abyss of despair or do you take one more step which is sure to change your life forever.

Are you tired of feeling beaten down by life, or feeling blocked because of the things that haunt your past? Do you find yourself fearing the faith step that you know is sure to catapult you to another level of seeing, being, and living?

My friend it is when you get to the point where you are truly sick and tired of being sick and tired. When you get a glimpse of the deep gulf to which you may fall and be lost, that you indeed realize that whatever it takes, whatever it takes! change must! come and it must come now.

I know and believe that these words are reaching out to someone who understands exactly what I am talking about. Maybe you are reading this and saying that is where I am right now, and I am hungry for change, hungry for the new thing. You are looking and yearning for the clearing of the clouds that linger. Are you looking for that brighter day? I'm reaching out to those who have been running hard and still struggling to stay ahead of the past. To those who have discovered that it is possible to be saved and still need deliverance, or struggle to live in total freedom. To those of you who have painfully found that you can be delivered and yet not fully healed. For so long many have been made to believe that when we give our heart to the Lord everything in our past, as well as the effects of those things, magically disappear.

Yes, when we surrender our lives to the Lord, we do become brand new people on the inside. The Holy Spirit gives us new life and we no longer see the world as we did before. The Holy Spirit gives us new lenses from which to view our lives, purpose, and direction. We become what the Word says, a new creation now living in a relationship with Christ. We are as it were starting a new life under the guidance of a new master.

All of this is certainly true. However, nowhere here does it say that the effects of our past life are suddenly eradicated. It is, I believe, the reason the enemy has caused many Christians who struggle to doubt themselves, questioning their salvation.

The truth is that for many, our new life in Christ gives us the opportunity and strength to begin working through the possible residue of past issues. It is a chance to free us in the present from the past and catapult us into our God-ordained future, with no condemnation or guilt.

Many people including Christians are wondering why they feel so stagnant in their journey. Why it is that though they strive and do their best to push through challenges there seems to be something that prevents them from going forward to another level. They wonder why it is that there are moments when the hurts of the past, the disappointments, and the memories that were pushed aside seem to creep in, just as they are about to excel and cripple them in the present. Could it be that they have been delivered and yet, not fully healed?

In, (1 Samuel 17) we read the story of little David and the giant Goliath. It tells of a nation being crippled as they cower afraid of the giant that is facing them. They know the stories of his fury and the thousands he has killed. They know the terror that he has been able to instill in the hearts of the people. Though these are people of God, anointed and appointed with an assurance that God had already said the land was for them. They would first have to be willing to face the giant that is standing before them with all the terror he has brought from the past. Only by doing this would the people of God be brought into the future which God had for them.

The people were at a critical place, on the brink of a breakthrough yet what stood before them in the present, reminding them of the past, could have kept them from reaching their future. Had it not been for one young boy who was not afraid to face the giant.

It has always been fascinating to me that when David comes along his fear if there is any, is overshadowed by his trust and faith in who God is. Knowing what God can and will do. David is an example of one who could see the facts yet trust the one who he knew to be the truth. The facts were that Goliath was indeed a great warrior who had slain many, and who held the people of God in fear each day as he came out to challenge the God of Israel. The fact was they had good reason to fear. He was great, and no man was a match for his might.

The truth, however, was that God was greater and that God would deliver this giant into the hands of David. It was a new day. David had a sincere trust in God and therefore did not conjure up a strategy for a sneak attack. In fact, the Bible says that David hastened out to meet the giant full-on, face to face. He Didn't try to reason with him, but called him out for what he was, an uncircumcised Philistine, no match for God!

Oh, what faith, what trust can arise when we are at a point of desperation. So, I say again I hope that this book will talk to those who have come to a point of desperation.

You are desperate for the great future that God has for you. You have had a glimpse of the future, you feel the unrest in your soul and you are now ready to do the work to position yourself for the blessings of God, freed, delivered, healed, and made whole from the past.

My journey to this turning point was a long one. I became a born-again Christian in my late teens. It wasn't long before I was spirit-filled, growing, and sincerely serving the Lord to the best of my knowledge and ability. Still, there would come a point in time when I knew that there was more for me. It was wonderful to be away from the life I had known before that point and to be emersed in this new life in Christ. For me, it was a safe place of belonging where there was love and acceptance, where there was God to watch over me and protect me from any harm. I had found inner joy and a sense of purpose in serving and being a part of a ministry.

It must also be said that the Christian journey does not come without its challenges, struggles, and even offenses in the body of Believers. My journey was not without exception. After all, we know that we wrestle not against flesh and blood only, but powers and wickedness in the spiritual world. Our God is often patient with us as we grow from babes in Christ to maturity. The day came when the Lord spoke into my spirit that He not only wanted me to seek to be holy but that He wanted me to be whole. I'd been grounded for years and thought I was doing well. I was on the right track so what could that mean?

Suddenly there was a flood gate of long-forgotten suppressed memories that kept coming back to me. I could be in the middle of praying and a scene would come to mind that would reduce me to tears. Anxiety would arise and for just a moment I was thrust back to the little girl I had long left behind, locked away in the closet of my mind and soul. Only now the spirit was knocking asking to come into this oh so private suppressed place. What could I do? What should I do?, What would I do? What will you do as God pricks your heart? It is my sincere prayer that as you read my own story of release, healing and complete, freedom, you will be blessed and stirred. This is written to encourage you, whatever you are facing, whatever your past has been, the ghosts that lurk in the dark places. The ones haunting you in your mind, my friend you can trust that God will NOT fail you. He will not leave you, and He will not harm you. You can be completely freed, you can be whole!

Food for Thought

Before you go on reading just pause for one moment.

Are you ready to possibly face some giants of your own?

Are you ready, will you dare to open every door or chamber and allow God's light to shine in every corner of your life?

He did not come to condemn the world but that the world through Him might be saved.

Your new life will cost you your old one.

It's going to cost you your comfort zone and at times your sense of direction.

It may cost you relationships and friends.

It may cost you being liked and understood, but it doesn't matter because the people who are meant for you are going to meet you on the other side.

And instead of being liked, you are going to be loved.

Instead of only being misunderstood you are going to be seen.

Then you will see that the only things you have really lost are those things which were built for the person you no longer are.

When we are filled with God's strength there is nothing that can stand in our way. <u>Adapted from The Mind Journal/ Brianna Wiest.</u>

Prayer Point

Lord, today I ask for Your courage to take this journey to a life of freedom and wholeness. Though I feel anxious and maybe even fearful of what I may encounter along the way as You uncover me. I know that I do not walk alone. I know that You are a healer. I know that You have promised in Your word that Your thoughts towards me are for my good and not evil. I will trust You and pursue the process. So, I ask that You lift my hand, hold my heart, calm my fears, bottle up all my tears and walk with me through this storm until I come into the full light of Your freedom.

Amen.

1
Chapter

A CONVERSATION WITH GOD

*I*n this search, I found myself in a season of unrest. It felt like the edge of desperation. I was hungry with what felt like an urgent desire for God, for strength and covering that could not seem to be quenched until it would be truly satisfied. But how would that happen? What would it take? Wanting God more than anything I felt an urge within me and I began to pray.

"Lord give me strength, for me to live as Christ and to die is gain. Open the recesses of my mind, go deep into the very core of who I am and bring me out. I give You permission. I need You to reveal any secret hidden thing, any door that has been shut to You, and any area I may have failed to release to You. Lord, do what You must. Shake this nagging in my soul telling me I need to move from here to there. I don't know where there is Lord.

Do what You will. I do not care about the pain that may come or what I may have to endure. I want more of You, more of Your power and I need Your anointing."

Tucked away in a room at a dear sister's house, for three days I tried to pray more, to describe in detail to God (as if He didn't already know) what I could feel brewing in my spirit. I often wrote or drew when I needed to reach deep inside myself and pour out my feelings to God. I read inspiring books on prayer, opened scriptures, and looked at various stories. At times just staring at them intensely as if something would jump off the pages, it would all just sink in by osmosis. Then the light bulb would come on giving me the answer to my unrest.

I sat there hour after hour. A sheet of paper was taped on the wall waiting for inspiration to hit me, so I could, at last, convey to God what I felt inside by drawing. Still, I waited and waited, every scribble was being erased. It wasn't right.

Then I began to draw, pulling pieces from the images I had seen, trying to format what was in my mind into images that could represent the essence of my cry, I kept drawing. Suddenly through the tears, it began to take shape. I found a sketch in an old art book. It was of a man on a throne. I didn't know who the artist was or the inspiration for the rendition, but it spoke to me and I continued to draw. After completing the figure on the throne, I just stared at it.

There was an intensity in his expression and his gaze penetrating. Still, there was one thing missing. I continued to draw, scribbling, erasing, scribbling again, trying to pour out my very soul until the picture of where I was in my mind would come to life. When I finally stepped back the tears began flowing as I finally saw it. I saw what had been missing.

It was me curled up before the Lord at what I would describe as His mercy seat. When it was done, I sat there staring at the drawing, waves of emotions and a hundred and one feelings surged through my mind and body. Scenes in my life played over and over flooding my thoughts.

One more final touch was needed though, so I picked up my tools and continued. On the figure of the girl, I placed small slits in the skin from which tiny drops of blood would seem to come oozing. For me, there was more going on than the figure bent over or curled up in despair. This was deeper than that. You see she was not only wounded, she was still at times bleeding, but no one would notice the wounds on her. You would have to get extremely close to her and search carefully to be able to see them. You see, these kinds of wounds are subtle, often invisible to the naked eye, yet they are there, exposing a deeper story that she dares not tell...Get close, get really close and you will see.

Sitting there staring at the completed work and contemplating, it was as though time and the world around me stood still for a moment as a deep sigh escaped my lips. It was at that very moment I realized that it was just me and the Lord. With this visual of God looking at me, the darkness surrounding me, and the tears of my truth beginning to flow.

I began to write!

Take My Hand

Strange, isn't it when there's so much inside to say,

that you don't know where to start or to begin.

What you feel seems so much stronger than you can find the words to convey.

You know you want to say it.

You know you want to be free.

In despair you crumble, wishing it would go away, those secrets of the past.

And Jesus says **TAKE MY HAND ANYWAY.**

There is a child inside us all you know, wanting to be free, to be loved,

A mother's hug and a father's reassuring smile,

All those things you think of and yearn for.

You stand to walk and then you fall.

Then sensing God's presence you call out of your pain.

Father have I failed You, have I let You down again?

Don't look at me that way.

Please stop!

For through Your eyes I see my shame.

In Your eyes, I see Your pain.

I am not worthy,

Sin's now my fault too.

Still, the Father gently says,

TAKE MY HAND ANYWAY.

How can You stand by and watch me die?

Don't You hear, don't You see all the tears I now cry?

How can I stand, how can I go on?

How can I even please You, when I am not pleased with myself?

Love You as I sometimes struggle to love myself.

If only I could win the war and never lose a fight.

If only I could soar as the eagles do in flight.

If I could run this race,

If I could pray,

If I could leap to new heights

Or still, just make it through today, make it through tonight.

If I could truly see You and know You, I mean **REALLY KNOW YOU**.

But I am afraid I'm just too far.

I see my filth yet need Your grace,

Here I fall before Your face only to hear You say.

My child, my child, have you not felt or seen how my love for you has grown?

I sacrificed all that you might not fall.

All that you desire I have for you.

Strength, blessings, my anointing, power to serve and grace to make it through,

If only you would understand I am here closer than you think.

All I ask is that you **TAKE MY HAND.**

By: J.W. Pratt - *December 1996*

Food for Thought

God is concerned about the things that trouble us, believe that. How glorious is it to know that God sees us, knows us, and still desires to be in a relationship with us?

Jeremiah 31:3 NKJV

I have loved you with an everlasting love; Therefore with loving kindness I have drawn you.

Prayer Point

Thank You Lord, for Your love. Thank You that You not only walk with me, but You hold my hand in Yours. You cover me when it feels as though I am far from You, you remind me how great Your love is.

I come to You now and I bow my heart lower than my knees could ever be. Here I am at Your feet, Lord please hear me.

You know my past You see the unseen wounds, You draw me close to Your table and in Your presence, I know that I can find true rest. In your presence, I will find true healing.

2

Chapter

THE SURGERY BEGINS

What could I say? other than here I am Lord, here is my hand. It was then, that the surgery began. I did not know just where the journey would take me. I only knew that I was not willing to let the secrets of the past haunt me today and keep me from my future. So, it was then that the doors were unlocked and the little girl, now a woman, began the journey of a lifetime.

I could not have imagined the twists and turns that this walk was destined to take me on, nor could I have imagined the pains, the hurts, the disappointments, the isolation, the tears, and losses that would accompany me on this journey. I was determined to persevere and not to give up. I wanted all that God had for me and I wanted it desperately enough to fight. On this journey, there would be great awakenings in my spirit, many talks with God, and visions to encourage me along the way. An anointing was released into my life, spiritual insight was given, to not only guide and comfort me but to protect me.

Maybe you noted that the drawing I'm referring to and the poem that proceeded was written in December 1996. This is just the way my journey went, like an onion, layers that would have to be revealed and peeled, and like an onion each layer peeled would bring the sting of tears, these layers were going to take time. Looking back there were times when I wondered why it took so long. Granted I am sure now that some of that time was due to my procrastination and inconsistency in obedience. Lessons that I seemed only to learn after I had fallen down. Then I recall all the amazing things that took place during that time. People I was able to connect with, the hundreds of souls I was able to minister to and help because somehow there would be a knowing in my spirit and God would use this vessel in ways, I cannot take any credit for. Oh, don't get me wrong there were plenty of heartaches and disappointments, difficult moments and tears. But there were also those times of great revelations, mercy, anointing, and even more mercy and oh so much outpouring of God's love. Lessons that I could not have learned had there been some quick fix. I would not have appreciated the journey had I not had to press through the process to my progress.

Even in the waiting, God was teaching me who He was and revealing Himself to me in my life.

While flying home to England one year I remember looking out of the window at the clouds hovering over a beautiful sunset and thinking. Here thousands of feet above the ground the majesty of the skies just commands Your respect, their beauty heralds the epic message of a creative majestic God. The only one by whom all things were made. Each cloud is distinct and yet they fit perfectly into the place God has put them. Even here God was going to teach me another profound message, as my heart began to pour out to Him while I silently gazed out the window. In my heart, I began to speak.

"God, I ask You to show me how to love the way You love, and yet my life has been filled with heartache and betrayal." Straight away I hear the words.

"That is so you might truly know how to love."

I continued, "I ask that You bless abundantly so there is more to give and yet I keep running into lack. The response, "That is so that you might truly know that I am your source, I am your provision. Even in those anxious moments I already know your need. Have I not always supplied your needs and more?" I had to smile and just rest in His peace as I continued to look out at the vastness of His greatness. It wasn't that God wanted me to live with constant lack in my life or never know love and peace. But it was to allow me to understand and truly appreciate His provision and timing in ALL areas of my life. To love when you are not loved is not easy, but it is what exemplifies the real heart of Christ. To experience peace when all around you, things are crumbling is to understand, you can and must trust God to carry you. He will not let you be swallowed up. That gentle reminder of His nearness would come back to me many times over the years, just at the moment I needed it to, and again I would remember the powerful lesson in the skies and smile.

Food for Thought

Sometimes it can be easy to forget how great, how vast our God is, and just how much He cares about the minutest things in our lives. If you ever take a trip on a plane you will see as you soar, the higher you get the more you see how perfect His creation is. There above the clouds, on a clear day, take a moment to see His majesty, see the peace, or just look up the next time you take a walk and take comfort. The Creator of heaven and earth is watching over you.

"The heavens are telling of the Glory of God, and the expanse is declaring the work of His hands. **(Psalms 19: 1 AMP)**

Prayer Point

Lord, today remind me to look up.

Show me Your splendor.

Give me a glimpse above and beyond where I am,

More than what I can see.

You have not lost control.

You are bigger than my past.

You are brighter than my present and will be even more glorious in my future.

Amen!

3
Chapter

THE QUESTION: TO BE LIKE CHRIST?

That same spring of 1996, I felt an unrelenting hunger for God and desire to experience the true transforming power of God that would make me like Him. Oh, I know we as Believers like to talk about how we are His, but as I read more and more of His word I wondered if what I did and more importantly, who I was truly reflected the God I said I served. I had met so many so-called Christians who knew how to talk the talk, knew the right moves, or cliché lines to say. They had as we would say in Pentecostal terms the 'Shout down packed,' and yet seemed to have no problem wounding a brother or sister in a second with their words or turning into a bitter ogre when they were not recognized publicly for their deeds.

My hunger was not just for the actions of God, but the mind and heart. "Let this mind be in you which was also in Christ Jesus." (Philippians 2:5)

I wanted the literal translation of this verse to be real in me. At this time I was living on a college campus and in my final year of an undergrad degree. Each day for two weeks as I went to pray, I found myself only able to cry out these words, "Lord I want to be like you." With those few words ringing from deep within, the inner spirit cry was opening my soul, asking God to check my very motives, what is the truth of why I do what I do even for Him. I wanted my heart to be pure in the service I rendered.

While everyone was asking, "What would Jesus do? I was asking what Jesus would think of what I did and how would His heart feel. Finally, one afternoon after those two weeks of crying out the same heart desire, I lay crumpled on my dormitory room floor sobbing at my Father's throne. Suddenly there was a soothing warmth that could be felt in the room, through my tears a picture appeared in my mind's eye. This picture was not one of spectacular glory nor a man robed in white with a halo and bright lights shining around him no sounds of harps. No! What I saw was the cross. There on that cross, I saw a close-up vision of Christ. His eyes were heavy, bloody, barely looking up with the weight He was carrying. The flesh on his face was torn down to the pink meat with fragments of bone peeping through. Blood weeping from the gashes that ripped, distorted, and disfigured his face. His eye sockets are so bloody and swollen you can barely make out His eyeballs let alone a pupil. His shoulders contorted as they are stretched beyond their limits. Pieces of skin stripped. His body was bruised with colors of black, purple, and green. I see pain, immeasurable pain, and agony. He has been beaten. Hatred, ignorance, and sin have spat at, rejected, ridiculed, and despised him. He had been dealt with treacherously. Mans' love had betrayed Him, so-called friends were all gone. He is left alone in this hour of need. With this vision facing me I begin to cry even more. I know that He was there for the redemption of all mankind, but at this moment, it became oh so much more personal. He is there on that cross baring it all for me. His eyes are looking at me, into me. I see Him and He sees me looking at Him. Then came that still small ever so gentle and questioning voice asking, "Do you still want to be like me?" For a second it truly felt as though my heart had stopped beating and that I had been brought to a critical point in my journey where I would need to decide. This was not the picture I was used to seeing. Did I mean what I so earnestly had been praying and crying out for? You Know there is a saying be careful what you pray for. Well here was my answer facing me. Would I be willing to go through, to bear the unknown? Was I willing to suffer, understanding that in this life of serving Christ we may encounter pain, disappointment, and even periods where it will feel as though we are carrying an unbearable weight of the world? There may be times when the road is filled with sinkholes that appear suddenly, and you will be about to buckle when it seems like it is all too much. Instantly as time stood still in those few seconds the words of a dear song came to mind. "Must Jesus bear the cross alone and all the world go free, No! there's a cross for everyone, and there's a cross for me.

It felt as though I only had seconds to answer the question that was still burning into my soul? As I looked into the eyes of Christ on the cross, I could not deny Him, this was after all the moment I had been praying about knowing Him, really knowing Him. That would mean knowing Him not just in the power of the resurrection but the part we so often forget, the fellowship of His suffering. I knew I could trust Him, I had to trust Him, and so I found my lips exclaiming with a great exhale of breath, despite the unknown, "Yes......!" Right there a blanket of warmth covered me as I lay there motionless, I felt the touch of His overwhelming love afresh and I knew my life would never be the same. Still, I was assured with the words that His strength would be made perfect in my weakness, (2nd Corinthians 12 V 9) and that I would be alright.

No weapon that was formed against me would be able to prosper, (Isaiah 54v17) But that He (God) was more than able to keep what which I had committed unto him that day (2 Timothy 1v12).

I knew that with him I was destined to be more than a conqueror through Christ who loves me. (Romans 8 V 37) What took place that day was more than I could have imagined, or even realized at the time. He was preparing me for the things he knew I would have to go through. That day grace and mercy took my hand and became my very best friends and I would come to need them more and more as I walked this path, finally to be freed and healed, made whole from

"THE GHOSTS IN THE CLOSET…"

Food for Thought

Are you committed to truly knowing Jesus even if that means times of suffering? When you count the cost make up your mind will you still choose Christ? Longing for God is the very breath of our souls! It is yearning for God with all our hearts that opens our souls to breathe in the spirit of Christ and live for Him alone. When we search for Him with such reverence the promise is we will find Him. Nothing is more important to our lives than longing for Jesus Christ.

Adapted from Soul Shepherding by Bill Gaultiere.

Prayer Point

Lord today I seek to know You and to see You. Not just Your glory but give me a picture of the true price Your love paid for me. Jesus Savior of my life may Your strength arise in me. In times of suffering help me see You knowing Your strength is perfected in my weakness. Deep to deep let my heart ever soar with You on wings of flight. Let me not be afraid to experience the fullness of You. Even if that means moments of suffering for the sake of the Gospel. Let me be willing to run, let me be willing to rise, lead me to that place to be more like You.

Amen!

4
Chapter

THE PASSING OF TIME

Seasons came, and seasons went. My life began to open in so many ways. I was beginning to flourish in ministry. I witnessed many souls coming to the Lord through my preaching. ME PREACHING! that in and of itself was more than I had ever imagined or desired for myself. Never did I think that I would stand before people and speak.

I can honestly say that each time I stood and began to open my mouth, though I had prepared as best as I knew how, the Spirit of God, in His mercy would intercede and minister through me. At that moment there would be no fear. There was a surge of energy and many times a sense of knowing, feeling intensely the needs of the people. Not only did ministry for me begin to enlarge but it also began to intensify. I would be aware of specific individuals, their struggle, and their need in that moment, and the Spirit of God would give me an understanding of how to minister to the direct need of that person. There was an acute awareness of the spiritual atmosphere and activity. Each time this would happen I was humbled even more knowing God can use whoever He chooses, my only true heart desire was that He use me, that I will be willing and ready to put self aside and go or do or say what He would bid. So, there I was preaching, teaching, singing, and writing, trying to remain in a place that I would be an available vessel God could use.

Let me pause and take a moment here! I want to encourage someone who is considering whether they want to be truly sold out for Christ. You may sense the Lord calling you to move to a deeper place of intimacy with Him. It is absolutely okay to feel nervous about what that might mean, what changes may need to be made, what habit or habits may need to cease, what unhealthy relationships may have to end. Go ahead and count the cost if you must, consider it all carefully, however, when you put Christ in the balance with anything else He will always outweigh the very thing you think you have to hold on to. That which you think is so valuable and you just can't do without will fade into the background. When placed next to the abundant blessings and future God has for those who are willing to truly, wholeheartedly seek to follow Him, everything else will fade. Please know your present pain will not last. The current darkness will not overwhelm you; you can trust God!

Meanwhile, in my walk, several events brought me to a place where I knew God wanted to elevate me to another level, and this would take a radical leap of faith and trust in God. I did not and could not have known what was around the corner, but I could feel Him pushing me as if it were toward a precipice.

One evening after being out in the summer sun I noticed as I wiped my brow with a tissue that my face was peeling. Not your normal dry flaky skin, but I was pulling off thin strips, some a centimeter wide and maybe two inches long. I didn't know what was happening and for the next few days thought I could remedy it by using extra moisturizer. That wasn't to be the case. Instead, that just caused it to have a burning sensation. I was sure it must be an allergic reaction to something, maybe my soap. So, I would just use cold water which seemed to be soothing and I hoped it would pass.

Well, while trying on an outfit, in a major shopping area a few weeks later I was wondering why the sales lady was looking at me a little strange as she showed me to the changing room. Stepping inside I was horrified and embarrassed when glancing in the mirror, I saw strips of dead skin hanging from my face and neck, talk about being mortified. Needless to say, after this point I sought the medical advice of my doctor who recommended a dermatologist. The doctor asked several questions and thought that it might be one thing, but after new symptoms of sudden swelling in the knees, legs, face, and ankles, weakening appeared, I was sent to a rheumatologist and then an infectious disease specialist. After about a month of prodding, poking, and testing the conclusion of all four doctors was lupus. What lupus? I didn't even know what that was at the time and even asked them how on earth did I catch it? Like I said I knew nothing about the disease. Right away I was placed on 60grams of prednisone as well as three other medications daily. This was a shock to me, and I quickly found that as my health suffered so did my ability to do the things I used to do, or I knew God had called me to do.

I had been given the privilege of ministering on a regional level serving some 52-churches through Christian Education and Children's Ministries. Sharing the heart of God for equipping people for effective ministry. Teaching and facilitating workshops is still one of my greatest joys. God had been moving mightily and somehow in my spirit, this setback did not sit well. I knew this was not where or how I was to remain. This sickness was often making me weak and unable to move. My immune system was so weak I suffered from bronchial pneumonia four times in that one year, each bout was worse and longer. The last one had lingered for three months. I was constantly in and out of work. It got to the point where they wanted to hospitalize me, my very life was now in real danger. This struggle went on for almost two years. Then one Sunday morning as I stood ministering in front of a group of young people in a children's church, something happened. Now, this thing had happened many times before in all kinds of places but, never here. I can remember thinking, 'No! no! not here, not now, please...No, No!'

Then it began, first I felt the heat in my body, I knew my temperature was rising, I could feel my face and legs beginning to swell the skin getting tight. I saw the troubled, scared expressions on their faces as I paused and held myself up onto the podium. I knew my face was turning purple and expanding before their eyes as it had done in previous episodes that year. Feeling somewhat embarrassed at not being more of a rock, I nodded to one of the other ladies to take over and excused myself quickly, planning to sit in the vestibule and get some air. The service was just about over so I would be able to go home and deal with this. However, God had another plan that day. As I came out and climbed the few steps into the vestibule, outside the main sanctuary doors, my legs gave way and I fell to the ground. Two of the young people told me later they had been concerned about what they saw and had followed me out of the room. When they saw that I was near to collapsing, they quickly ran over with tears streaming down their faces they tried to lift me, asking if I was okay.

I knew they wanted to help, and I could not even help them, to help me. I was so weak I could not even speak. Here is where I broke, and the silent tears began to fall, no sound could be heard, just silent tears. I was tired of these sudden attacks that would leave me weak and in so much pain. Those of you who suffer from this debilitating disease or know someone that has it may understand. Then there was what I would see in the eyes of those who witnessed the transformation as my skin changed from caramel brown to pink and then to purple, or while my fingers, legs, and face literally changed shape and size before them. The fear, the pity that I saw in the eyes of those looking on was more difficult than the weakness and pain my body was experiencing. For almost two years I had put on a brave face, not letting anyone know how difficult it had truly become, pushing ever so hard to still be there, not let anyone down, not give in to the pain and discomfort.

Today however I was done, exhausted, and almost ready to give in to the illness. I was tired of the overwhelming sense of helplessness. Tears silently rolled down my cheeks. There were those who knew I had not been well and that I was getting treatment, but they did not know to what extent. The team of four doctors and I were working on it. I always tried to not let anyone see me during these episodes as I didn't want them to see my weakness. I had become like many of you reading this, the wounded healer pouring out to others, giving, being the rock even while you are in need yourself. Sound familiar? So often a trait of those in leadership.

Not today though, today it was all out there. Not knowing what else to do one of the young men went to get help. Less than ninety seconds later two of the deacons were hoisting me into a sling seat they had made by locking their arms together underneath me while my arms went around to grip the shoulders of the towering men on either side of me. Never will I forget the atmosphere as they carried me through the sanctuary doors and down the aisle. The singing and motion turned to still silence. Heads turned from each aisle as we passed by. You could hear the sounds of people gasping at what they were witnessing, caught off guard and surprised. It was clear many of them felt almost as helpless as I did. I was brought to the altar where a chair was rushed to meet me, and I clung to the sides trying to stay as upright as possible.

As my Pastor approached, I looked up at all the faces and the eyes that were now looking at me, every eye. It was undeniable that these were people who cared. I could feel their love trying to reach out to me. Some stared in disbelief faces grimaced, as though they were feeling my pain. There was a strong spirit of mourning that seemed to come over the place and as I looked around the church I can remember being drawn to a group of young people. These were youth I had spent so much time with and ministered to over the years holding onto each other, the sound of tears and sobbing permeated the atmosphere. My love for them wanted to hide them from seeing me this way.

By now two or three of the nurses present had stepped forward my clothes were being loosened, and temperature taken as they insisted that I be given space to breathe. Apart from rushing me to the hospital, there was nothing they could do apart from giving me my medications and waiting for this episode to hopefully pass.

At least that would have been the case. But today was going to be different. I was broken, yet remarkably, faith within me insisted on standing up tall amid people of faith. It dawned on me, there was no better place for me to be at this time.

The Word declares that, He was wounded for our transgression, He was bruised for our iniquity the chastisement of our peace was upon Him and with His stripes we ARE healed. (Isaiah 53:5)

I had read, heard, preached, and taught this verse hundreds of times before. Used it quickly for colds, aches and pains, and minor ailments; and yet in that moment, it was about to become more real to me than I could have ever imagined. The sanctuary echoed with the sounds of crying, moaning, whisperings, and the prayers of the saints as the Pastor rested his hand on my shoulder and said quite simply.

"The Lord is not finished with you yet," he said, but it was enough to stir something in me. Something that said you are not defeated, God can handle this. You shall not die but live and declare the works of the Lord, Amen!

Lifting my head up I remember seeing two or three streams of what looked like winged lights circling high above my head. At that moment I knew that this illness though it threatened to kill me was not what it seemed. I can only explain it as my spirit man understood at that moment that this was not just a physical ailment, but a spiritual war had been waged to derail my path, throw me off course, knock me out. I had only dealt with it in one dimension with earthly physicians, just accepting what they said without much question, after all, the evidence was there for all to see. Now it was time to fight for my life and strength not only physically but spiritually. I could not recognize it at the time, but I did know that if my path to God's purpose for me included this season then I was going to make sure He would get the glory even in the midst of it.

For the first time, my focus was not on being healed but on being willing to let go. I needed to go through whatever came my way for His glory. At that instant I rose from the chair and almost immediately collapsed to the floor of the altar, my knees overwhelmed with the amount of edema (fluid) that had gathered. The words 'For Your glory,' began to well up on the inside of my being. Over and over again I repeated those words as if sending out a defiant message into the atmosphere and to every principality, my victory had come.

Now the words were being said out loud continually as I crawled across the length of the alter. This test was now my testimony, to all who were observing this illness; this season would not steal my joy, my praise, or my faith. Indeed, each declaration seemed to beget more praise, more praise gave more strength until I was now on my feet, hands raised and tears of determination flowing. Rousing praises of encouragement filled the auditorium. The atmosphere had become almost tangibly electric. Yes, it was glorious, and I would love to tell you everything disappeared straight away, and we all went out dancing. Don't get me wrong that day I certainly did go out dancing in my spirit. Even if my body at the time did not show any physical change, I had been changed yet again. Now I was learning firsthand, (2 Corinthians 12:9 AMP)

"My grace is sufficient for you [My lovingkindness and My mercy are more than enough—always available—regardless of the situation]; for [My] power is being perfected [and is completed and shows itself most effectively] in [your] weakness."

This was just the door being opened for the lesson that was to be learned, there was a process to my purpose. Sometimes to get to your destination you must go through unfamiliar, sometimes uncomfortable terrain. Still, a miracle had already taken place, in my spirit, I was convinced of that. During the next few weeks as I prayed, I continued the mantra, 'Lord, for your glory.' In my heart, I was convinced my outlook on this sickness as merely physical had to change. There was now a need to war in the spirit for my complete healing from this diagnosis. The following two weeks it seemed as though the episodes came more frequently and more intense, yet each time someone asked how I was doing, my unrelenting answer would be, "I am healed," followed by, "My body just hasn't got in line with my spirit and testimony YET!!." It was interesting to see the strange looks I would get as it was obvious, I was in pain or that my body was transforming before their eyes.

Still, reminded that this was to be a spiritual fight I was determined to speak life, to stretch my faith, and to speak those things that are not as if they were. Faith after all is the substance of things hoped for, the evidence of things not seen. (Hebrews 11:1)

Everything I now spoke seemed to go against the evidence of what was being seen and what had been tested. Each test I had undergone every skin biopsy and blood test. Lab test had only confirmed the diagnosis that I was suffering from Lupus. Yet here I was speaking and declaring the opposite. At the end of those two weeks of praying and declaring, the Lord spoke to my heart concerning a matter I thought was completely unrelated to this struggle I was facing with my health. Yet, God was about to open another door of understanding.

Food for Thought

Just when you feel as though you want to give up. Just when you decide that the struggle is too much. God will step in to show you that He is with you. He is closer than you think. Those that will worship Him are admonished to worship in spirit and in truth. The challenge and truth of our worship must be that in every circumstance of life we are willing to surrender to the process of His purpose in our lives. And that we will, in the good times praise His name, and in the bad times do the same. Decide today to look up in faith. Don't be swallowed up in thoughts of despair. I promise you, your help is very present.

Prayer Point

Dear God, please give me the strength I need today to endure this situation, this trial this test. Guide me to the blessings and lessons that it contains. Help me to have the endurance to continue moving forward from strength to strength.

Guide my thoughts, words, and actions, so that even in this storm, I will walk in victory Your path of love and peace.

5

Chapter

A CALL TO ARMS

My friend, the spiritual realm which we cannot see is real. The power of words is real and the spiritual fight for your soul is real. God was about to teach me another principle of spiritual warfare. Often, we feel we must fight our battles alone in secret, but there are times when what we need is a helping hand of a brother or sister. We are called to lift one another so that we walk not alone neither harbor the secret attacks of the enemy.

As I began to ask God to show me how to battle this sickness differently, I remembered that there was an individual who had been displaying some disturbing behavior towards me. I wasn't sure how this could have even been connected to this illness until I began to replay what had been going on. In short, I had ministered at the local church he attended several times as well as other meetings where he had also been in attendance. There were polite general conversations every so often.

Then came the phone calls suggesting that God told him I was the one for him. This caught me off guard and I kindly told him God had not said anything like that to me and that the idea was not something he should pursue; I was not interested. He seemed to understand but shortly afterward he began showing up at my place of work. The calls continued sometimes from different numbers and became even more strange with fanatical claims of him being the one God had sent to save the world. I would not answer but began to tape and write down what he was saying. He began to get agitated when I didn't respond, making claims that God had told him I would have to go with him to meet Jesus and then return. He claimed this was key to the plan God had given him and was to be kept as a secret.

His other statement was that God had given him authority over me and if I did not do as he said he would not be able to stop what would happen to me. As I said for some reason when these calls were made, I did not respond with a reply but felt lead to write down everything. There needed to be an accurate record of the things that were said. I did not know at that time how important that information would prove to be. Though I had purposely kept my distance from this person he had begun to map my whereabouts through friends and the district or regional church calendar. It was not too hard for him to find out what church I would be ministering at next.

This individual went as far as showing up at the workplace of my dear friend, Doreen a church sister and armor-bearer trying to find out from her where I would be ministering and if she would organize a meeting with me. When she refused and advised him to stay away, she was threatened not to interfere or something bad would happen to her.

Now almost a year after this had started, it was all coming back to me. I was feeling overwhelmed and not knowing where to begin other than to pray for clarity. Then it came to me, it was time to get help, to touch and agree in prayer with some prayer partners. After praying and following what I felt was God's leading, I made four phone calls. Two of those calls would be to two couples in my church who had become like big brothers and sisters, then there was Doreen the armor-bearer previously mentioned, and myself. I did this while saying to myself, "Okay, if this is really You God then they will all say yes even without knowing why."

I needed to schedule a meeting with everyone. I simply asked that they meet me the next day at a certain time. Without question, each one said yes even though they had no clue why they were being asked to come. This only reinforced within my spirit that this was indeed God's leading and the timing was now. When we came together it was not clear how to present my suspicions. I believed that my illness was a physical manifestation of the spiritual warfare for my soul and divine purpose in Christ. I was about to begin a spiritual cleansing of all the people and influences I had allowed into my space. In fact, it sounded crazy to me, but I knew that everyone God had placed in my spirit to call were all spiritually sound people who had a heart for God and somehow this would all make sense in their spirits. After praying together, I told them about the calls I had been receiving and read the transcript from my journal as they sat in silence. When the reading was concluded there was a heavy atmosphere in the room. Instinctively it was as though we knew what had to be done.

There are times in this Christian journey when you go through a difficult situation or season and all you need is someone to talk to, someone who will sit with you and just listen as you pour your heart out, someone to support you or even cry with you. Yes, there are moments when that is just what you need.

This was not one of those moments, what I needed were some warriors. There are fighters, there are soldiers. There are generals and captains, but a warrior is on a whole different level of warfare. When I think of a warrior I think of a certain level of courageousness, loyalty, experience, and skill in the art of war. They are active, relentless for the cause, and on the front line. I needed fellow believers who would be ready to go with me into a very real spiritual battle, to wage war, to go as it were into the enemy's camp and take back what was being stolen (My health).

We set up a twenty-four-hour prayer chain and talked daily to touch and agree, decreeing and declaring various scriptures and promises from the Word. With the prayer support of my brothers and sisters, I took another radical stand and shared what had been going on with my regional overseer. With my consent, he contacted the individuals' pastor and set up a meeting. When faced with being exposed this individual who had been declaring that he was the last days' messiah, and saw an anointing in my life, was convinced that God had picked me for him and thus had been given authority over me. Was nowhere to be found. Suddenly he claimed he was not allowed to speak because the overseer and the pastor would not understand. Sound unbelievable yet? Listen, the last thing the enemy wants is for his devices and deceptive plans to be exposed. When wickedness is brought into the light it will begin to crumble. I knew God was moving me in the right direction.

Now it was time for yet another leap of faith. Upon my next visit to the doctor, I informed him that I wanted to cease taking the medications. Let me take a moment and clearly state that this, of course, is certainly not advisable for everyone, and this thought did not go down well with my doctors. However, I had a strong assurance that this was the path for me to take, and so I stopped pumping my body with all the medications which were supposed to help me bear this disease.

Those who were standing with me understood that as we entered this battle each person could possibly come under spiritual attack. During the following three months one of the prayer warriors, the very same sister who had been threatened at her job, to not keep the stalker from getting to me, contracted a rare strain of bacterial pneumonia that landed her in hospital with a collapsed lung.

Symptoms of the disease that had almost crippled my life and stunted my ability to travel for the ministry continued to rear its head. Still, my testimony remained I am healed; my body just has not caught up with my spirit. Another prayer warrior had a severe almost fatal asthma attack and another almost lost his home. All the while we continued to declare and decree healing from unleashed spiritual infirmities and any other spiritual interference against God's plan and purpose over or, in our lives. At the end of three months, I was called into the doctor's office, it was time for another biopsy. It was not long before I received a call that the results were in and I needed to come in again. I can still remember the puzzled look on the doctor's face as he exclaimed.

"Ms. Waite, I don't know what to tell you, a few months ago we were ready to admit you into hospital for treatment. Today though the biopsy and blood tests have come back clear and conclusive; there is no trace of lupus anywhere."

All I could do was smile as I exhaled and continued to listen. "I have been conferring with your other three doctors and we all have the same conclusion that all traces have gone, this is quite astounding. We know it was here in the blood, but it is gone," he said,

Almost immediately the words came to me and I responded, "It was in the blood...your right! it was in the Blood of Jesus; the miracle was in the Blood of Jesus all along." They just looked at me and I saw the nurse in the corner of the room break a smile.

Praise God who is the truth and the light. What a lesson I was learning. God's truth is greater than fact. It was a fact that I had lupus. All the tests, all the symptoms said so but as I began to stand on God's truth and not my facts, things began to change. The truth I declared was that I believe with His stripes I am healed. I believed that my purpose was greater than this illness. It was a mountain and if pure faith could raise up, even to the size of a mustard seed, this mountain would be removed into the midst of the sea. I believed that if two or more could touch and agree, that what we bound here on earth would be bound in heaven, what we would loosen here on earth would be loosed in heaven. I believed that no weapon formed against me could, nor would any longer prosper. (Isaiah 54:17)

God had given me the power to tread upon serpents and if I resisted the devil he would have to flee. I believed and stood on the Word that one would put a thousand to flight but that just two could put ten thousand to flight. There had been six of us knit together in this battle. We stood united knowing that the weapons of our warfare were not carnal, but God promised that they would be mighty through Him to the pulling down of strongholds. Hallelujah! I can feel a shout of praise welling up right now just thinking about it. To think for those two years, I had simply accepted the diagnosis given without question. After all, they were the experts and I trusted them, without even consulting the Father each step of the way. After all, this was just my lot, or so I thought. How many of you reading this know that when God steps in everything in the equation changes? They were the experts but not the final authority. Whose reports will you believe? Do you even bring your ailments to the Father?

I almost withered away. At first, the enemy had me feeling somewhat guilty about sharing what had been going on. God, however, reminded me that, that is always a ploy of the devil. He uses secrets to hold us captive. The things this young man declared were unholy and dangerous they needed to be exposed; once they were exposed, he withered out of sight. God was teaching me another lesson in this, which was to whom much is given much is required. As the Lord anoints you for service you must learn how to discern and guard that anointing. Wise and timely words said to me from a dear Reverend.

Yes, it is true other believers are drawn to like spirit; however, the enemy of our souls is also drawn to that anointing, but for a very different reason, for the enemy comes only to steal, to kill, and to destroy that anointing. I was learning a valuable lesson, guard you're anointing, as naive as I had been at that time I would need to understand that everyone that was smiling in my direction was not always in my corner, even in the church circles I associated. That may sound harsh, but it is the reason God gives us the spirit of discernment. The tares and the wheat must grow together and will, until the day of God's harvest.

I am sharing these very real moments with you so that you understand there was no quick fix. There was, however, a process to the progress for my release into purpose.

The journey was just that, a journey filled with twists and turns as well as revelation upon revelation.

Food for Thought

When going through trying times we too often forget the power of agreement. For whatever reason, we become reluctant to ask for help, for fear that we will appear weak in the eyes of others. If only we would recognize that this  false thinking is what the enemy uses to isolate us, in the very moments we need community. My friend, there is power in praying together. Deuteronomy 30:32 tells us one can chase a thousand, while two can put ten thousand to flight.

There is still a multiplied stream of power that is released when two or more are gathered before the savior with a united focus. Prayer agreement leads to breakthrough.

Prayer Point

Lord, help me today to recognize when it is time to ask for help from a brother or sister. Lead me to those who will be able to come alongside me. Those who will step into agreement for this petition in accordance with your word. And Lord help me to remember that I am my brother's keeper, and not to stand in judgment of those who seek help to stand. Understanding that we are all part of one body, we at one point or another will need somebody to lean on.

Amen.

6
Chapter

THE ONION FACTOR

*L*ike an onion, God was peeling back layer, after layer, after layer. His quest! to get to the very core of my heart, to heal, renew, to free my heart. I had prayed earnestly declaring the desire of wanting to be like Jesus, to be covered in Him. I did not understand it yet, but my prayer indeed was being answered. God was going to go to the very inner chambers of my being. He was going to pull on all the broken pieces of my life. Every leaking place was going to be exposed. He would reveal and go to the darkest most painful places of my soul, not to punish me but to bring His light and healing which in turn released power.

Listen, God is concerned about ALL of you, not just a part. When we come into contact with the risen Son of God. When you have a true encounter with Christ, He makes us different, our lives change. Yet, it would be foolish to deny what we have seen or experienced in our lives. Time and time again some Christians struggle with the residue or effects of their past. Like those who may have experienced for years being beaten down verbally. They come to Christ and excitedly receive a new life, only to find so often that they continue to struggle with issues of low self-esteem. Or, the person whose internal wounds cause them to continue in a destructive habit that had become their coping mechanism.

The Good news here is that when you hunger and search to live in the righteousness of God, He is not going to let you hide from yourself.

Regardless of any self-destructive message I had ever received from others, God wanted me. That in and of itself blew my mind. He wanted me to be whole as well as holy, to do that I would have to be willing to allow Him into some painful shameful places of my past. I would have the dare to open the door and release the ghosts in the closet.

My dear friend it has taken many years, twists and turns, bitter tears to get to this place where I can write in such a candid way. There were good days, great days, and days when this journey got so heavy, I didn't know if I could take any more. The struggles were real and certainly not without lapses and many mistakes made by me. Still, God covered me, and many times rescued me from a pit of my own doing to protect me from myself and to preserve what He had placed within me. There were many layers that needed to be peeled back. Each one more difficult to peel, each one deeper and more painful. After years I would come to understand the work in me did not end with me and wasn't even all about me. It was oh! so much bigger and deeper. With that being said, I invite you to come with me at this time into the journey of my path to freedom and wholeness.

Food for Thought

So, you hold an onion in your hand and begin to peel back or cut into it. Before long, your eyes begin to water. The more you cut into it or press it, the more the onions expel the substance that was hidden inside. The deeper you go the more the onion tries to protect itself. But if you want to truly release the beautiful flavor of the onion, though it's uncomfortable and your eyes are streaming, you keep pressing, you keep peeling or cutting into it. One of the ways people often calm the effects of the onion is to run it under cool water. Placing it under the clear water calms the agitation of the onion and the reaction. The path to full healing and wholeness sometimes takes time. Though we may cry and want to get to the root, the truth is we are not always willing to fully open those hidden places all at once. It is often said that hurt people, hurt people. You will leak what is inside. God knows that your path to healing and wholeness transforms not only you but it directly impacts and can help the lives of those close to you. So, He will walk with you, waiting patiently for permission to be invited into each space. In this onion factor, as I like to call it the Master will skillfully, peel back each layer washing it clean as he soothes the tears.

Prayer Point

Lord, I know that there are times that I lash out at others and it has more to do with what is going on inside of me and not what they may have said or done. I recognize that I sometimes become afraid and anxious when I do not know if it is truly safe to reveal that hidden place of pain.

Lord as you have done for so many others, hear the cry of my heart. Help me not to rebel when You begin to peel back the layers and press. Help me to be confident in knowing that at each layer You will not only wash and make clean but that You have promised to cover me. I will not be left naked nor unprotected. What You have begun in me You will bring it to completion.

7

Chapter

LETTER TO A SISTER – PART 1

*I*t's October 4th, 2006 at 6:51 p.m.

"Today I am beginning to write. This has been a long time coming and though I was afraid, today I am excited and nervous. Some things I write here will be painful for both of us. But I am assured that it will bring about a release finally. Not only that, but the bigger picture is God is merciful. God is a healer; God still has a plan. For He says in the book of Jeremiah 29:11, **For I know the thoughts that I think toward you, saith the Lord, thoughts of peace and not of evil, to give you and expected end.**

I want to talk to you from my heart and I am praying that God gives me the strength to say everything that I need to say. I feel as though I have been on this journey for such a long time. I am tired, I am worn, and still, God has not counted me out, never! I have been stronger than I ever thought I could be, I have also been broken, alone, and struggled to understand my purpose. To know who I am meant to be or to experience what it is to soar, to fly. So, you see I need freedom and I need wholeness too. I understand that now.

So, today I am releasing the ghosts in the closets. Today I need to dare to unlock the door to that dark room. The one we sometimes keep in the secret place of our souls. It's the place we keep things hidden from our consciousness for fear it may engulf us, and we would no longer be able to cope or exist. It causes us to fear that everything we have held dear would crumble and fall away only to reveal that the pain of a wounded child is still residing in the very core of the woman or man we have become. Though we appear strong and whole we are inside broken, locked in that room with the pain and wounds of the past.

Earlier today on a break when I sent you a text regarding our childhood, I wasn't sure how you might respond. When I finally got your reply, the tears began to flow. Although I was standing there in the backroom library of my classroom, it was as though time had suddenly frozen. I quickly moved through the classroom, catching my co-teachers attention I excused myself and ran to the bathroom.

The inner little girl was about to burst and I needed a safe place to be alone. I thought finally I am going to be free. The secrets will be exposed. I began to thank God that he had brought us to this point now. This is so real. I feel it. We are on the verge of a life-changing transformation. I know it is crucial to do this now.

Later, I am going to share some things with you that I should have done a long time ago before mummy died, but I was afraid to. Today I am at a place in my life where I am so very desperate for the good God has for me that I don't care about my own shame. I don't care how much it hurts, or how unrelenting the tears are that fall as I pen these words to you. I have spent many days counting the possible cost. I want, No! I need wholeness, I want to live! I'm choosing abundant life.

My sister make sure you are sitting down, that you are comfortable and that you have already prayed first before proceeding to read this. Then hang on because we are about to burst through, tear down and destroy a domain of generational bondage.

I am taken on a journey back to a little girl who kept asking the question "Do you love me?" Do you care about me? The little girl who thought I need to be good. The little girl who didn't want to upset anyone. Do you remember her sis?

Nothing ever seemed to be stable or certain in our house, was it? Apart from the certainty that if mum and dad were there together at the same time there was going to be some kind of confrontation. If not, then the silence was going to be so thick, so deafening, so filled with a sense of fear, nervousness, and dread, that if he (Dad) should call my name I could already feel my heart begin beating twice as fast and not to mention the effect on my poor bladder. I would feel as though pee was going to trickle down my legs at any moment.

In my head, my only hero was you, my beloved sister, Dawn. I wanted to be just like you. You were the one that always seemed so strong, never showing emotions, no tears. You were always in control; you stood your ground and nothing or no one seemed to move you. To me you were fearless. I did not know it at the time, but I believe your coldness was your way of protecting yourself and maybe even me in your strange way.

All you had to do was come on the scene and it was as though everyone could tell that there was something special about you. Everyone loved you, admired you, and looked up to you. MY SISTER! I idolized you so much, whenever you were upset with me, I was crushed inside and would curl up and cry, everything you did affected me. At that time, I only saw myself, my worth through your eyes it seemed.

I remember once you were mad at something I had done. I must have been around eight years old and you used these words to scowl me. "I can't stand you! if you only knew how much I hate you." I can remember right then feeling as though my whole world had turned upside down at that moment. Those words pierced deep into my young soul. I went to that small corner, tucked away deep inside, and cried to myself. She hates me, my hero hates me. I can remember for the next three days I didn't speak, not because I didn't want to, my whole being was still needing to know you would forgive me and validate my worth again. I didn't speak because if you were possibly still mad at me, I didn't want to upset you again and hear your voice piercing my heart. I didn't want you to shrug me off or push me away; I didn't think I could take it.

Not until the third day when you ruffled my hair did I know everything was okay and I could now move around the house without being anxious and on eggshells. You never knew how much I was tormenting myself, wrestling with my inner self. All the while you just thought I was pouting.

Funny the things we remember! Our parents had so much going on, so much conflict and wounds. Emotionally and psychologically I could not depend on them and you were the one that became my world. The model example of a provider always wise beyond your years. A protector, throughout school no one would dare touch me because I was Dawn's sister, and everyone knew that you could and would fight if challenged. "Who's that?" I would hear even when you were not around at school. "Oh, that's Dawn's sister."

I don't even remember having a name. Think about it, to everyone around us, I was simply known as Dawn's sister or the nickname I acquired when I was nine years old (Bunggy!)

But who's that?

My memory went back to being locked in what we used to call the hole. Do you remember that little dark closet always seemed to be filled with cobwebs, no lights, just an eerie whistling wind? The one with that creepy attic door on the roof that we never opened but the wind would whistle through it like the chilling sounds of ghosts. That's where I would be locked up at times. It was your way of having a little fun I think because you knew I was afraid of the dark. There I would bang and scream and cry begging you to let me come out. As I listened to your voice on the other side of the door taunting me with stories about the rats that were going to eat me, how they were in there and coming for me. Then there were the big spiders that were there and the cobwebs that seemed to know just when to brush against my face.

Gullible me, even when I tried to comfort myself there and say it's not true, somehow your words had already got into my mind and stirred up the fear, though I tried to be brave and ignore the fear, it was true for me. After all, my sister had said so. Yes, we played as children and we just did not know how those games would be a vehicle the enemy could use to influence so many areas of our lives.

Mom from a very early age would tell us that all black men were no good, and not to talk to our father, not to play with him but to watch the way he touched us because he was a man and they all want only one thing. What a scary and confusing message to start hearing as a preschooler. It worked because I was always on guard around our father. I was taught that everything he did was suspect.

Dear Dawn, there were countless times, I would stand on the inside of the staircase, on those occasions when dad would be home. The door was already half shut, cracked just enough to see a portion of my face. Standing there I would say good night daddy in a voice, so quiet you could hardly hear. I remember the one where my lips hardly moved. He would say to come over, for a hug or kiss goodnight. Did I ever tell you that there were times he would kiss me goodnight on my lips, only it was not a peck or tap on the lips? But it would linger, it was wet and pressing. He would try to force his tongue into my mouth and then just laugh and play it off as I ran upstairs? I remember thinking I don't like that. I don't want any man to kiss me. Yuck!!! It just did not feel good, did not feel right in my five or six-year-old mind.

Then there was our mother, so wounded by her brokenness and unhappy marriage, desperately wanting the attention of a man that did not seem to even see her. If she was unhappy everyone was going to know it and be unhappy too.

Many times, I wanted just to be around you, but no. Mom said you were going to kill me, that you had an evil eye, that we couldn't be trusted together, that you were jealous and evil, in her words, "A big-eyed toad Bitch," to be exact. Those conversations would go something like this. "Mommy, can I go to the store with Dawn?" Only to hear the response "No! Dawn will push you into the road and kill you." I never believed that to be true and couldn't understand why at times she kept us apart. In fact, it only seemed to encourage you to play more pranks on me when she was out of the house. I remember you sitting me down in front of your friends to eat a plate of flies you had caught and you put ketchup on.

So many games, most of which seem to bring back what I considered the good times. Even though in the games we played they reinforced that I was always less than you, at least in my eyes. Remember our dolls, I would use my voice for your doll, and you used your voice for mine. Only my doll would always curse at me, call me names, and never listen to me. Once I got so enraged, I beat her, burned her hair, I even poked her eyes out. The rage and anger that would surface wanting to shut her up, remember? All the while my doll would keep taunting and laughing at me. Only it wasn't the doll, it was you, my sister that was talking, it was you laughing.

Then there were the other games. Secret games that opened darker doors. The ones when no one else was there. Clothes almost gone, laying there. Do this, do that, go back there, lick here, suck, touch, rub. Do it or else!

"Is it my turn now?" I would ask. Only to hear, "I did it already." Or, lay down let him touch you there, just stay still.

Sorry, my dear sister but I must go there. I have been there so many times by myself in thoughts that randomly invade my mind. I'm tired of the secret. I can remember that friend of yours in our bed who snuck in to play, and me keeping still and silent so as not to be in the way or to disturb you both. I can't be in the way and upset you. It was just games, just fun. It took me to today to now I understand, that doors had already been opened.

Later, I would find myself in a predicament. Mom was long gone to America by now and we had both grown. I was nine years old and you were fourteen when mom left. Still, I stayed in your shadow. My voice had no volume. Even for myself. What do I wear? Ask Dawn. What should I eat? Ask Dawn. Dawn knows. Please understand that I now know that was my insecurities and lack of understanding that allowed you in my eyes to be in this impossible place. I don't think you could have realized just how much my world depended on you. How much I needed you or how I was seeing my value through your eyes, as though your responses to me determined my worth. But when you are raised in a house silent in words of worth or affirmation, when there are few to no validating touches especially from your parents, there is a tendency to look for someone to see you, to recognize you, to pour into you. That may not have been fair to you I know. I must have been a weight to you at times, I just wanted to always please you, so you wouldn't complain or push me away. It didn't seem as though our parents gave us any thought. They were just too busy dealing with their issues.

At thirteen, fourteen you were the surrogate parent. At nine years old I can recall we both cheered silently when mom left for the States, of course, we couldn't make any real noise, but we knew as we looked at each other wide-eyed, standing there at the airport terminal watching the plane leave, not knowing when or if we would see her again. We both turned and smiled at each other. I genuinely don't recall feeling any kind of sorrow at her departure. How could that be!!

Maybe it was the relief of knowing that at least we would not have to listen in silence to the screaming and fighting anymore. We wouldn't have to see or hear her painful tears. We would not have to fear being beaten out of the bed late at night, to polish and shine the stone floors in the kitchen.

Maybe, just maybe, we would be able to laugh in the house together. We did not know it yet, but the truth was we were going to need one another more than ever.

We were always on edge not knowing what was going to come next, can you remember that sis? Without using words our spirits clung to each other looking for ways to get through each day, or just to find a reason to laugh, searching for ways to feel protected. It was our feeble attempt to make some normalcy out of the chaos that surrounded us.

It is true that by the age of thirteen or so those inappropriate hidden games had subsided, but the doors had already been opened, those familiar spirits were already at work. For all the things that had gone on in that house, the cloud of suppressive, distorted spirits hovered heavily. Fear, feelings of less than, and embarrassment had already taken root in the hiding place of shame, now protected by a fortress of guilt and secrecy.

Shush...don't ever tell!

Food for Thought

The foundations of how we process our world and our thoughts, begin before we can even verbalize those thoughts.

Children will always look to their caregivers usually the family unit for validation and a sense of self-worth. It is in these formative years that often doors are opened, spirits of influence, positive as well as those with destructive distortions begin to contend for the mind. As adults, we may struggle to understand why some things affect us more than others. What is often overlooked is what has been fed into the soul of a child.

Prayer Point

Lord, help me to know that you see all of me. You see the child within. My innocent cries have not been ignored. You know of the yearning to be loved and protected by those who should care the most. The things unheard of by those around me. I am lost in the secrets I keep. Lord help me to trust in Your love for me as You walk me to the other side of my pain.

8
Chapter

WEARING THE MASK

I had learned in those early years how to pretend, how to hide and tune out the reality of my world, and my own feelings. At school, I seemed to have the freedom to laugh that we didn't have at home. Not only that but I found that I could make others laugh too. It's quite amazing now when I think of it. How indeed did I learn that? How did I know just by being the center of the humor and laughter I could deflect others from really seeing me? It meant that I could remain invisible in plain sight. That's all I had to do to hide. Make them laugh, I learned; and I would never have to worry about someone asking how I was doing when they were laughing. What was I going to tell them anyway? By now my mother had been gone for a while. Was I supposed to say that at times there was no food in the house and hadn't been for days, or maybe I was supposed to tell them we had been on our own for days, hadn't seen dad, and didn't know where he was?

"A smile can be a mask we put on when we don't want to explain why we are sad and why we cry inside our hearts."

I hated going home to the cloud and heaviness that seemed to dwell there. No one dared to come to the house especially when mom had been around. They could barely speak to us on the street especially if it was a boy. All our friends were always scared of her. Then when she was gone it was the sneaking in and out, climbing out the window down the roof in our nightgowns or pj's, sneaking to see our friends, or bringing our brother's girlfriend to him.

As I grew, I just wasn't sure how to respond to boys approaching me? It seemed much easier I found to have casual friends but nothing more, boys didn't get much closer than that. I was more like one of the lads.

In the later years I discovered that if I liked a boy and he was insistent on trying to get my attention romantically and wanted to take it further by touching me, I would allow him to touch me without having me. I mean I could almost become a spectator outside of my own body. Take on a character, play a role. After all, I was good at that.

I had already learned what to do when we were children with the games we played. All I had to do was pretend, I was whatever he said. It was just another role, a game. I could know that his hand was on my leg or thigh but feel nothing. I convinced myself that he's not touching me; just the shell. My brain would be saying, 'I'm inside and you can't see me or have me. You can't touch inside of me.' I would go numb.

The mind is an amazing thing, the enemy of our soul is indeed seductive and deceptive, and in those moments! In those moments I could almost convince myself that I was safe hiding inside of myself. You see you don't realize until later in life that as you misuse your body or allow others to misuse you, it wounds your spirit, leaves cracks, and tugs at the very essence of your soul. Building on the distortions, reinforcing the secrecy, guilt, and shame.

You see the door for the spirits of lust, shame, guilt, worthlessness, unworthiness, and yes even death, to operate had been opened years before as a four-year-old child. The confusion of what love looked like or what you allow this distorted concept of love to do, can destroy a life, and now they (lust, guilt, shame, worthlessness, unworthiness, and death) had a right to be there.

I remember finding and reading with fascination one of the books my sister had hidden, 'Man and Woman,' I think it was called. The book described in detail all about those erogenous zones and what could be done, at thirteen years old, it was a lot to understand. I found my brothers' porn books, extremely explicit ones, read those too, I knew where he hid them. Which only gave me yet another set of lies and distortions. In one particular book, I read how I could now be what one of the articles described as a professional virgin. You didn't have to have intercourse, you could do other things. Which was only adding to the distorted truth of my worthlessness the person without a name of her own, described only as the one with the long hair or Dawn's sister. I would often catch myself continuing the narrative in my mind adding, you mean the weak one? The one with the big bottom, full lips, no need to take her seriously, and no one did.

Even with the crazy messages I had on my sexuality, there was something in me that wanted to try and keep something for myself. At sixteen I was already feeling peer pressure from my boyfriend who just seemed frustrated because I wouldn't have intercourse with him. In my mind, I could hear Mom's voice saying, 'I told you, you slut.' I felt the very real struggles of wanting to be cared for, protected, and seen as worthy of love more than I saw in myself. No man could say they had me, even if they had touched my body.

For so long my sister was my hero. I struggle even these many years later as an adult. How might she view me after reading my letter? Would I be strong enough to be without her if that was where this all brought us to? I had to trust God. After all, it was He who had stepped in and shook my very foundation and it is He who is pulling me, pushing me into a new destiny. All those years I spent smiling on the outside meanwhile I was searching and screaming on the inside.

The little confused girl inside of me was always there in that dark, quiet, silent room. She had nothing to say, at least nothing worth hearing. I could see that room in those times when my mind would go off searching for meaning and purpose, and physically feel the manifestations of the spiritual oppression saying, 'You are NOT to be heard.' Then to reinforce that I found that when I was upset because I was not ranting and raving no one took me seriously. Some people would even try to think up things to do to see who could get me to lose my cool. They wanted to discover whether if I got angry enough, would I fight. The truth was I don't think I knew how to, or I was afraid that if I did explode or went to that dark angry place I would lose myself in that darkness or become trapped like I saw my mother and father.

The shouting, the fighting, and the fear were only one piece of the home they had created. I think the hardest part was the absence of any sound, the deafening silence. No laughter or giggles, as young children, no playful banter. No family discussions, no signs of affectionate touch. At least not if one of our parents was present in the house. Our stance was to tiptoe around, always look busy, better be cleaning something, stay out of their way, don't ask for anything, do not be heard. I think that I was afraid that I wouldn't be able to come back from that angry hurting place, I had seen so many times before. Then there was the incessant teasing of my body parts from home and school which dug scars deep in my psyche that reinforced my warped self-concept. Even though of course I laughed about it. The only thing that was important to me during that time was that I had my hero, my big sister. My sister was the only consistent, dependable thing in my life.

A Turning Point:

Forward 1986; there we were at Aberdeen Street Church. Your boyfriend of seven years has finally convinced you to go to a service and of course, I must go to. We had talked and we made a deal, no one is pulling us up to the alter. We knew how those Pentecostal type churches are. We both agreed that we knew what we believed.

Yet before I know it, you are at the altar and I'm left thinking what on earth is she doing? I mean what is this? I thought we made a pack. I was doing what you told me. As we are leaving the church, once again, I have faded into the background of your shadow. Observing from the outside, it seemed like person after person came to hug and congratulate you on your new life in Christ. How could you leave me on the outside when we made a pack?

Now you're smiling and saying how different you feel inside. I can tell something has happened to your spirit. Your countenance changed as the tough you had disappeared and you were in a new place. I can't let you leave me, I thought to myself. I knew I would have to find my way to that new place too so that we could stay together. If you are there it must be good so, 'God show me,' was what I kept praying as we left the building. I felt the difference and separation between us. Not because you said something, I just felt it.

The following week, all I can think about is God. The next week you were unable to go but I decided to go back alone. I don't even remember what the message was I just wanted it to end so I could go to the altar and ask God to come into my life.

There I was seventeen years old, a new babe in Christ. I was told all things were passed away and everything was new. The trouble is no one remembered to tell me how to operate as this new person when I was going back to the same clouded place to live.

How could they? When they didn't know the old person. They had no idea where I had come from or what my past experiences had already ingrained into my being. I wasn't even fully aware, but I did know I wanted this God who they said knew all about me and still loved me.

I was excited that now we were more than sisters by blood. Still, we never talked about the secrets of our childhood. We don't talk about the fact that at home we still struggle with feeling emotionally and psychologically unprotected.

How uncanny that even there at church I would be known as your little sister. I've come into the light, yet I am found only in your shadow. "Who's that?" someone would say. "Oh, that's Dawn's little sister," would be the reply.

Always the second thought, the third glance. You have always been so strong, took care of me, kept us together, stood in front, and protected me. When you enter a room you are an undeniable silent force.

A few years later you got married. I can still recall the tear in my heart and soul as those words rang out. 'I now pronounce you husband and wife.'

"Wait a minute this is not supposed to feel this way," I tell myself, but it does. Something ripped a part of you from me, and me from you. We had always been together, leaning on each other. We covered each other; we were inseparable. We couldn't afford to not get along, especially after mom left and we became so much more to each other. You were my mother, sister, friend, counselor, everything. I thought Tony was just going to be joining us. But when the preacher said those words, 'You are now husband and wife,' especially in that moment my soul knew better, I felt you leave me even though I was standing right next to you. I knew that I would have to change positions. It was no longer me and you, it was you and your husband standing there, starting a new life.

I just knew that I wanted you to have the kind of happiness that I had heard about in God's Word and that we never got to experience in our parent's example. I wanted you to have what we had come to see in the church family. They had so quickly taken us under their wings and in as their own. Tenderly known as mom and dad, Beryl and Danny Roach.

Do you remember just after our conversion they invited us to dinner? Good thing because God knew there had been no food in the house for days. It was the first time we had seen a family all sit together and eat. The first time we had witnessed a husband and wife in playful laughter or affectionate touching. I remember following her hand with my eyes as she sampled an item from her husband's plate. Never saw that before. Their two daughters laughed and talked with them at the table. Such a foreign yet beautiful thing.   Remember that night when we got back to our house. I was seventeen and you were twenty-one years old by then. We didn't say a word to each other when we got inside. We just sat there in the living room, held each other, and cried for hours. After the hours had passed, we still didn't say anything, there was just silence. You said nothing about it, I said nothing. As always neither one of us explained why there was such a reaction in us. Did you have the same feelings of despair that I had? Did you have a sense of being lost, somehow feeling cheated? So, this is what it was like to grow in an atmosphere of love and laughter where you were secure and safe, everything we had not known. Just sitting there at dinner, I had been soaking it all in.

The impact of that night we both knew would remain with us, throughout the rest of our lives. Now you were married, and you would be able to create your own happy, loving home. I still could not have known God's plan for my journey was about to go into full swing.

Food for Thought

There is a Japanese quote that says, 'You have three faces.

The first face you show the world. The second face you show to your close friends and family. The third face you never show anyone. It is the truest reflection of who you are.'

God's love is powerful and has a way of seeing through all the masks we wear. Reaching to the deepest core of who we are and lovingly drawing us to a place of naked acceptance. His love covers and receives, reaching into all our broken sacred places as we surrender to the loving Father. It is then the true transformation begins, and we must trust in His guide to find our way out of the shadows to live in freedom without the mask.

Prayer point

Lord, I have worn a mask for so long. I am not sure who I am underneath. Help me today Lord as I trust in Your love, to take off this mask as I speak to You let it be without hiding my broken places. As I receive Your Word, Your direction, encouragement, and strength I know that You are with me and will show me how to live in freedom anew. Thank You Lord, for loving me to life.

Amen.

<h1 style="text-align: center">9</h1>

Chapter

I NEEDED TO GO

ere is where it all begins to go in a different path. Remember we said we would always be together and even live next door to each other, just like our imaginary childhood characters did. We thought that was exactly how it would all happen. Yet, there came a time when it was I that needed to go.

Mom had been in the States for more than half my life by now. Every year we were being promised that she would be sending for us, until we stopped hoping, stopped asking about it, or believing it. She was constantly saying how bad it was that none of her children wanted to go and live with her, that she was getting older and needed some company. Then out of the blue, we get the call, our papers are ready we can go! It should have been a time of excitement, but things had changed. However, dear sister, you were now married so that was out of the question.

Our brother was never easily found anymore and was doing his own thing. He had found his place of belonging in martial arts and a group of people he called brothers and his path did not have room for us it seemed. So, I was the only one that was left, and I was unattached. I knew it was time to go. You insisted that I move in with you and your husband when you got married. You didn't want to leave me in that dark house alone. I knew I needed to leave for you to draw closer to your husband and not have me there as the crutch. You needed to be forced to build on your marriage not, hide in it.

Fast Forward:

I moved to America and I'm trying to get to know this woman that is my mother in a more intimate way than I knew her before. From a nine-year-old child to a twenty-one-year-old woman is a big difference. Oh, the battles we were having. Then there was the big cultural shock coming from England to the States, but I wanted to stick it out. I reconnected with a dear friend Russell, who I knew back in England and had migrated the year before. We instantly connected and spent most of our time together. We created a great bond, what I might call a sister's pack. We attended the same church, sang, and traveled together.

She's such a breath of fresh air, outgoing and carefree. We always seemed to find something to laugh about and it was easy in some of those difficult times in my mind to hide behind the laughter. I didn't hear any of the ghosts of my childhood calling me I had no idea they were still there. After all, I was now saved (Born Again) and I was told, everything old was now past and behold I was completely new.

Someone forgot to tell me that for there to be a new you, you must be able to release, let go of what is old, not just physically but psychologically and spiritually. I still held onto that insecure little girl. I still had the occasional flashbacks when I could remember things we had done. Flashbacks of pictures brought nothing but shame and condemnation to my soul. Oh, I thought I was strong, by now I was no longer in my sister's shadow. My sister was not here so now it was as though for the first time people were seeing me. Or, was it me? The truth was they saw only what I showed them or told them. It appeared as though I was fine, a pillar of strength to others just like my sister was but that little insecure girl inside of me did not feel strong, she was still longing to be seen, loved, and heard. It got to a point that whenever I saw the girl inside I became angry at her for being so weak, I didn't even want to see her or hear her, and I certainly didn't let anyone else get close enough to see her. I didn't want the story she might tell to be mine, yet she was me. God this is hard to write even now. Don't get me wrong I'm not crippled or bound any longer. That is part of the victory God has given me. I do, however, at times mourn the part of the innocence of being a child that she missed or was lost to her.

A year or so after being in the States someone comes on the scene. He wants to get to know me, but I am truly nervous. I prided myself on being unavailable, keeping my distance.

Always in the back of my mind were the images of the fights between my parents, the tears, the hurtful words, emotional wounds that had been the example and foundation of my young years. There was still that little voice that would remind me of my mother's warnings, "All men, especially black, are no good."

I would tell myself I know the deal, not interested, don't get involved, protect yourself that was my motto. The truth was I was afraid that I didn't know how to protect myself. I struggled with wanting to please everyone and not disappoint anyone. There was a fear of not wanting to be pushed away. My thoughts again were still warped. Anyone who has ever lived this way already knows this is certainly not a healthy way to live. Still, I told myself if I don't let myself get close, I can't get pushed away. My thinking at the time was if I don't fully trust, I won't be disappointed. It was safer to just keep it as just me and Russell, my long-time sister friend. Different characters for sure but we blended well, we both supported and respected the individuality of the other. It's not always easy to find a friend you can remain close with for a lifetime. We are each other's British connection in this strange place. I told myself she never has to see my tears or hear about my inner struggles if any. I can forget about the little girl inside and be someone else here and that suites me fine. Russell is the social butterfly usually upbeat, we always seem to find things to laugh about with little effort, our humor is in sync.

On our many excursions, we kept bumping into this man at concerts, conventions, and more. Finally, we make a connection and I agree to go out with him for his birthday. I am nervous and excited to go on a date. And he's a charmer. Well, for the next two years or so we become more and more attached. He loves me at least he tells me he does, and I believe him. He says he wants to marry me and that he believes he finally found the woman God has for him. All along I'm thinking, 'Could it really be my turn to be happy?' I want to open my heart to the possibility. Maybe I can finally let down my guard. He meets my mother and tells her that he loves me and promises not to hurt me. I talk about my sister so much that he feels compelled to write to her, introducing himself and telling her his intentions toward me. He is not afraid to tell everyone who asks how much he loves me. Loves me. Wow!

I couldn't remember being in a place where I wanted so much to hear those words this way and now that they were, for me, they were life-giving. I certainly had never been in a place where I could receive those words. It had always been too scary, too much to even contemplate. I attended a popular church denomination and he is well known in the circle of churches. As the seriousness of our relationship became known among the churches, people began calling me. I notice there are whispers to the side when some people see me. "So that's her, the British girl," I overhear them say. How is it that even though I had left England and came to the States and doing well for myself, I still didn't seem to have a name? I was not in my sister's shadow anymore I was in my own shadow. On the outside, bubbly and full of laughter, on the inside still having nights where all I could do was cry out to God in the aloneness, always stopping short as soon as I saw that little girl inside wanting to raise her head and plead her case. She represented the shame of what I had done and experienced as a child and allowed others to do to me. A reminder of how weak I was along with all the images I still struggled with at times.

Now if you wanted to know who I was, I was often described as one of the British girls as if we were some kind of novelty. When I think of him though, I think to myself this is such a beautiful feeling to be loved this way. I can love him too. He had my heart; he had my attention. But how do you truly do that when you have never been taught what that means.

So, my thoughts were love never hurts the object of its affection, and you always put that person first. So, that was what I tried to do, I must accommodate him, put him first and I reminded myself not to argue because when you argue then that person may get mad, and when they get mad, they shout and fight, then that someone leaves. My warped solution was don't disagree with him, accommodate. "What's that dear, you want to go full-time in the ministry?" I'll start thinking of work that I could do to support us both if need be until we are in a better place. You want to move to another State. No problem, I'll just put off finishing college for now and get ready to leave. You don't want to see me wearing that or this, no problem. The thought I operated in was to put all his thoughts, wants, and feelings first above my own. One may say noble, that's exactly what love does, it puts the needs of the other above yourself. Maybe, however, this cannot be at the cost of losing yourself. Could it be that I was hiding behind him?

Then came the blow from out of the left field. As I greet his father at the ending of a church function, he says to me in no uncertain terms, "You are not good enough for my son. I have invested too much in him and he's going to minister. You have not finished college yet. If you both want this, then you will have to go beyond and above me, and frankly, you don't have what it takes. I don't think that you both have experienced true love." I don't know if there was a mic drop, but I do know my heart dropped. I felt as though I had been hit with a hammer. I wondered did he just see me as a novelty, British girl in America. I was wondering did they just like the accent but didn't know much about my family, so that put them off? However, it was all conjecture, as I was informed that it had nothing to do with my nationality.

The church was closely intertwined and some families had what seemed to be a more elite position than others. So here I am, being told that I am not in the same league. They came from a family with a long history of ministers and have a lot of history in the church.

I was standing there hearing the words but not being able to speak or move, knowing that I was indeed ready to commit to the son of this man. Confirmation yet again in my warped psyche, I thought, 'You're nothing even others can see it. Your worth is little, you don't even have a name.'

As I find myself lost in negative self-talk, the father walks away, and I felt literally stuck there to the ground. Later that evening as I sat dazed all of the emotion and tears begin to gush. I had held it together, made it out of the building, drove back to my room, head spinning in a thousand and one directions. My heart pounded so hard, what had I done to offend this man?

But there is a hope his son loves me, he said so only four days ago before he had left town for a few days. I decided not to tell him about the encounter because that would be like pitting a son against his father, asking him to take a side. I can't do that.

Soon he will be back, and he will stand up for us both. He will let them know the truth that he loves me. And then we will wait. We will spend more time together to allow his dad to be at ease so that he can give us his blessing. He'll see I'm not bad, I'll be the daughter he never had and love him. Honestly, I have so much love to give to someone, I'll make them laugh and when they are old, I'll help to care for them. As a couple, we could push back any date and hold off on any immediate plans to allow our love to prove itself.

But what I got two weeks later was a 'Dear John' letter. Janet, you're not the one for me, he wrote. Just like that the love he declared was somehow gone and I couldn't understand it. He felt there was no need to hear from me or talk to me first, not even face me. My thoughts on the matter were irrelevant the decision was made. During that time of waiting to hear from the man I loved, I wrote, I listened, and I poured out to God. It's what I do when I can't let it out to anyone else, I write to God. This is what came out of my soul.

Journal entry November 6th, 1990

Dear Lord,

You have always been there for me in good times and in all my times of distress. Right now, Lord feel my sadness, confusion, and distress. I know, oh Lord, that only You can fully understand what I'm feeling, thinking, and understand what I am going through. You are my only consolation and I know You will be there from everlasting to everlasting.

God, I just have to talk to You. I need the peace that comes from You, and I need Your comfort. I'm not sure what is about to happen, but God give me wisdom and grace to speak, to move, and think as You would have me to. Give me patience and most of all strength. Why can't I restrain these tears? LORD! LORD! LORD! Hear me. My head is pounding, and my eyes are puffy trying to hold it all in, but I cannot. I need you, Lord.

One hour later there is a stillness here, my head still pounds but I managed to cry myself to sleep for an hour. I buried myself in Your words, when I awoke, I looked for anything to distract me from the present pain, and anything that would give me comfort, peace, and hope.

Although I tug, I must be willing that THY perfect Will be done. I tell you Lord that I am once more afraid, and you say:

I have not given you the spirit of fear but of love power and a sound mind. 2nd Timothy 1:7

You tell me that everything will be alright, I hear your voice saying, "Use this as a time of purification, of rededication, of listening, of hearing, of communing with Me. I will not let you down."

Funny as I look back on it now, God was preparing me, and I didn't even know it, not yet. And so, I shut down and worthlessness began to speak.

"Why should he talk to you?" said the little girl locked in the room of my soul. She had dared to come to the door and peek out, dared to open her heart, only to be yanked back in and shoved into that corner. Three days of crying with my friend Russell and my Pastors wife keeping vigil. No food, no drink, no washing, no work, just questions. Every card, photo, or letter he had written was on my bed for those three days. I read them over and over trying to find where it had gone wrong. Why am I never enough? What is wrong with me? Some young girl or woman reading this right now, you know the exact feeling I'm talking about, 'Unworthiness.' For the next fifteen years, I would live with a closed heart to love as if punishing myself for being gullible.

What had happened was my fault and I deserved it? And then I stopped, and as I had done so many times before I closed myself off, I simply shut the door to my heart. Some wondered will the British girl run back to England now, I mean I had close to fifty calls asking just that question. Not so though! Our relationship was widely known, now his sudden departure was being talked about. I knew I would have to face the inquisitive faces, the looks, and the stares. Some looked with pity at the woman who had been abruptly tossed aside. Some seemed angry and disappointed for me and others just whispered and pointed.

I however wanted to, no I needed to, STAND. God had shouted quite loudly at me saying, "I was there with you before this young man. I was there through the tears and I am still here now so stand strong in Me and let Me take you to the place I need you to be. I have already told you I will not let you down so trust me." It hurt so much, still, I needed to stay even closer to God.

So, I continued to sing in the choir, while I cried at home. In the quiet moments I wrote, then I wrote some more. Eventually, I wrote a play, and it seemed to help me to get out some of what I was feeling. I wrote all the songs and then took that play on the road. In a small way, it was like therapy for me and so many others were able to identify with the truth of the production. The play highlighted the fact that we all at one time or another have had masks that we sometimes wear. One of the songs from the play, 'Still Be Loving You," is my song of confession to God. Did God see the pain I was going through? Did he see the tears I'd cried? The resolve of the song echoed this thought, no matter what would come in my life I was determined to still pursue and hold on to my love for God. It was my testimony, my love song to the Lord that I would not give up. 'Work It Out,' was another very personal cry. The song says, 'Work it out I know You can. If I but trust in You, You'll see me through. Lord work it out I know You can, Lord I put all of my troubles in Your hands.'

It was all a part of my self-therapy. During this time, I am saying to God I accept the call on my life. It was not to be fulfilled blending silently behind a husband's ministry call as I had thought, but he was calling me. ME! God was going to give ME something to say. He was preparing ME, God had anointed ME.

He saw me and kept trying to tell me that I had worth. I just couldn't hear or believe it. I was still carrying in that dark room the baggage from my childhood. I was hungry for something more. I couldn't put into words what exactly, I just knew I had to believe despite the hurt, the disappointment, and pain, God loved me and knew what was best for me. Around this time, I move onto campus at Nyack Christian College. This place was to become a catalyst into yet another sphere of understanding. A divinely intentional journey that would ultimately challenge me to the core. It was my sanctuary, a place I would not have to deal with the looks of pity, the talking behind my back, or the whispering in my hearing. It was situated just far enough outside of the city to offer breathtaking peaceful views of the Hudson River from the campus set high upon the hills of Rockland County. I thought I was there to study, seek God, get clarity, exhale and regroup while preparing myself in ministry and the workforce. I should have known just by the miraculous way things quickly aligned, housing, finances, and classes in my favor so that I was able to attend. It was clear that God had something far greater in store. This was going to be an eye-opening season that would bring me to the beginning of my transformation.

Food for Thought

We do not always know the bumps, the potholes, or indeed the twists and turns we will encounter in this life's journey.

Some we will see and be able to take a deep breath as we brace ourselves to lessen the shock of the impact.

Others we will not know are there until we feel the painful impact scorching through our hearts and souls. In those seasons where your world seems full of sudden uncertainties. It's hard to see at the time but it means anything is possible.

Prayer Point

Lord, help me to remember always that when I am caught off guard or knocked down by the disappointments in life that You are right there. You know when to hold me, when to cover me and when to carry me. The language of my tears You understand, they are not wasted, You hear the content of every drop. Help me to see while I am worrying about tomorrow You are already there waiting to meet me with all that I need.

10
Chapter

HELP! MY ESCAPE WAS A SET UP

I remember the man who God would use to begin yet another turning point in my journey. Professor Paul Staump is a Christian counselor. There I was in my counseling methods class, I listened to him intently as he went over the syllabus. Everything that was shared in class was to be confidential. He would be conducting group counseling and each one of us would have a partner to practice with, to counsel, and then to be counseled. The idea was if you weren't willing to deal with some things, then don't attend the class. This was going to be good I thought to myself except for one thing. So, at the end of the first class I calmly but quite confidently walked over to this rugged-looking man yet pleasingly approachable, kind of hippy looking with a pony, and I say, 'I'm excited about your class sir and I'm more than willing to keep things confidential and even counsel. But I don't think I will be getting in the chair." His response was, "Cool, okay."

I thought well I'm glad we got that settled.

For the rest of the semester, he never pressured me. We had some pretty moving classes that left us in tears at times, as one of the students would become the counselee for the day and the professor would skillfully begin to peel away the layers of their life.

Without being able to help it they would begin to tell of past hurts and present struggles. As for me I stayed intact in silence, took it all in, often going back to my room and telling God I do want to be seen but I don't have the strength to show myself, so God see me.

I continued to stay on the outskirts, always looking in and observing. At times even giving what I thought was insightful input. Until that day when the tables were suddenly turned. There were only three weeks left of the semester and there I was reliving the events of some five years prior. I wasn't even in the chair, He (the professor) simply asked my thought on a situation that had been presented. Before I knew it, he was peeling me. Speaking and reaching past my face to my inner crying soul. There I was still heartbroken over my jilted love. It was bottled up inside of me. I couldn't cry at church because everyone was already saying poor thing, pity she has no family to speak up for her. Or they would point, "Is that her?" Or, they would just come up to me from all over the country at different events with that look on their faces. Wherever I went, whatever state I was in, people seemed to had heard about the British girl cast aside, who was not worthy of the Bishop's son. They would walk up to me touch my hand or shoulder and just shake their heads in pity. Even if I wanted to, it didn't seem to be a safe place to be able to forget.

Russell and one of the other girls started acting like bodyguards. I couldn't cry at home because my mother would clutch her heart and say that it was too much for her, and I should have known that I couldn't trust a man. Day in and day out she ranted and raved about going up to see his parents so that they would know that I was somebody's child.

"Just because you were alone in the church didn't mean you weren't somebody's child," she would say. I can understand her wanting to protect me, but I already had an assurance that God was taking care of me. I needed to maintain my Christian witness. I was determined to walk in integrity with my head up. And to pray that despite the hurt that lingered only love would resonate in my heart for those who had so carelessly disregarded my heart.

Meanwhile, my dad came over from the UK for what was supposed to be a meeting only to find me locked away in the room. He then proceeded to say, "Look what you did. You let this man come and make a fool of you. If you had used your common sense (his favorite line in all things) then you wouldn't be here like this right now. I can't stand foolishness," and with that, he booked his return flight to England and within a week was back home. No hug from a father, not once did I hear how are you doing baby? Or any kind of consoling words. It was my fault. That was all there was to it and suddenly at that moment, I wished I wasn't so weak.

Anyway, on that day in class as Professor Paul conducted yet another group session, he asked a question and was talking to one student when suddenly, as I said, it switched to me. What about you Janet what do you say. I don't know how he did it but there I was. Recounting the following episode.

Months after my love had left, I finally needed to ooze, and I just needed a place to cry. I was at home, so I knew that was not ideal. But I couldn't stop it. It was bursting on the inside; the tears were pouring without my permission and I needed to be silent. My mum was in the next room and the last thing I wanted was to have to deal with her raised voice pointing at me. So, when I realized that my hand over my mouth was not stifling the groans coming from deep inside, I crawled under the office desk that was in my room and clutched myself in a fetal position. I just needed to feel me, to find me, to comfort me. The little frightened girl suddenly wanted to scream out. She could not contain it any longer. She had been abandoned by everyone that meant anything to her.

My mother said she loved me, but had left by the time I was seven, returned a year later only to leave again when I was nine, this time for good. Dad never told us he loved us, but I just guessed he did because he's the father, but he was never there. My sister loved me, but she had moved on to married life, so as good as gone. My brother had immersed himself in his world of Martial Arts. We barely saw or heard from him then. Then there was this man who I had opened my heart, said he loved me too, but now he was gone.

It would be safer not to love anyone I then concluded. While I sobbed and looked for comfort, I heard Mum's voice. She was looking for me. 'Come on Janet get it together.' I told myself, as I was cowering under the office desk in my room shaking. She even came into the room but when she didn't see me, she left. She kept calling my name and looking for me. I couldn't answer; I kept trying to stop but it was too late this volcano was erupting. Just trying to keep my breath steady was a task. Finally, on the third time entering the room she notices me under the desk clutching myself, knees bent, and my arms wrapped around myself in a fetal position. It was what I needed. I just needed to feel me, to let me know I was there still standing firm. Mum lets out a cry, clutches her heart, and raising her voice she says, "What are you doing to me, baby? My heart! Please stop! Don't you know when I see you like this, you're killing your mother?"

So, I did. Just like that, I stopped. Stopped crying wiped my eyes, and came from under the table to listen to her rant for the next two hours about how I was trying to kill her. Because seeing my pain was too much for her. I couldn't help thinking, why couldn't she just reach for me, pull me out, hold me and tell me it will pass, it will be alright, and that it will get better. Instead, I was the one causing pain, so I stopped; I stopped feeling, so she wouldn't feel the pain. I didn't matter, I would stop so I would not be hurting her.

After recounting this story in what was a very matter-of-fact voice. Professor Staump looked intently at me and said. "Who taught you that?" I was kind of caught off guard. "Taught me what?" I replied.

"Who taught you not to feel?" Just then class was over, but those words would thump at me. Some five years later I was still cold, and the truth was I didn't feel, no one was getting in, no warmth, no one to affect me ever again. Being closed was fine. Back in the dorm room, I sat, cried, and told her off for speaking. That little girl had no business opening her mouth about me. For some reason, I was compelled to draw. As my hand moved across the paper it was as though a cocoon was opening. For the first time, I saw her, not just in my mind's eye but physically on paper, sitting there in that fetal position in the corner of a black room. It was a closet, my hidden closet. You wouldn't even notice her unless you looked extremely closely. How that mimicked my life. She had no name. She didn't even look up and no one looked for her. The door was locked with chains. I don' know if they were put there or if she put them there herself but she did put the reinforcements. It didn't matter who put them there she was not supposed to speak, she was supposed to stay quiet, stay in her place.

As the picture of my soul began to creep to the surface my anger turned toward the professor. I was so mad at this man. How dare he open this can of worms with just two classes left until the end of the semester. How could he? What was I supposed to do with it now? I'd show him that was the last time he would get my guard down.

Food for Thought

Sometimes we try to find places where we think we can blend in and where no one will notice our pain. Deliberate smiles and being busy may help us drown our inner cry but try as we might that does not stop the cry. God sees us, God hears. There is a purpose as He guides our steps.

He cares more than we sometimes realize. Though we think we cover it well God can allow someone to see past the smile, stop you in your track, and speak to your soul.

So, do not be surprised if the place you thought was going to be your escape, turns out to be the place that was already prepared just for you. The place where you are challenged with the opportunity to step forward, find your authentic self. Your true voice and strength to stand up. The place of your escape can turn into your place of release!

Prayer Point

Lord I know it is difficult to try and hide from myself because everywhere I go, I find in this mirror of life I am faced with me. The pains, the secrets, the fears are right there with me. They creep into my dreams and my moments of silence. It is even more futile to think that I can hide from you. Yet I do try.

Thank You for preparing a place where I can encounter Your grace. Even when I think I am walking in my strength and have succeeded in camouflaging the wounds and memories, You go before me to let me know that no matter how far I go, no matter how deep I fall, no matter the distance I try to run, You will make Yourself known. You are there, Your love is there. You still see me. Hallelujah! You still see me.

11
Chapter

LETTER TO A SISTER - PART 2

A Journey from Wellness to Wholeness
Sunday October 22nd, 2006 at10:27p.m.

*H*ere I am again Dawn. I will try by the grace of God to continue this; God please help me! So much to share with you my sister, stay with me you will see that this was all necessary.

As I said that day after the class, I was compelled also to pick up a piece of paper and to draw. I had no preconceived thing in mind, just wanted to draw. Through tears, I began, but it wasn't long before I was finished and there she was, just as I had seen her in the recesses of my soul's eye. Deep in the shadow, pitiful, and in that dark corner, I had seen so many times before. I saw her and knew it was me.

Still, when I finally saw her, I could hardly bear to look at her! Angrily I tore it up as if to silence her presence which had become apparent.

The next two weeks of class were hard. He did give me his card to maybe go for some one-on-one counseling. Although it never happened and I went back to ignoring her once again. Some things took place in the next few months that are certainly key, however, although they are important in this process that God was taking me through. I need to leave them out, for now, to get to what is the pinnacle for both me and you Dawn.

The year before mom died, I had walked into yet another class that was going to change my life. This time I was in seminary Graduate school and taking a preaching class with Professor Martin Sanders. There he was looking like some Harley Davidson biker, six feet plus, big and burley, ponytail, beard and all. I sat there at the back of the class as I always did in all my classes, silent, low-key. He was very charismatic, down-to-earth, and humorous with a wealth of knowledge. I could tell that I was going to enjoy this class. For some reason, at the end of the class, as I was leaving, he stopped me at the door and said, "It's Janet isn't it?"

I just thought he was trying to recall the names of the students as they left. When I nodded, he continued very matter of fact, "Can I talk to you for a moment? There is something about you and I believe God wants me to commit to helping you. So, I want you to write down your struggles, dreams, and goals in life both spiritual, temporal, or educational. Bring them in with you next week and I am going to try and see how I can help you get there."

At first, I wanted to laugh at him. I thought what a strange man, he surely cannot know what he is asking. I have so much stuff going on inside me he's going to be sorry he asked and I'm going to give it to him. Now you must understand that as I said this is a year after the previous episode in my undergraduate studies class, so this time I was going to be on guard. I was not stirring the pot this time. I was going to write down so much and be real, I wanted to see if he was for real. I'll pour it all out, he'll back off. He won't know what hit him.

Well, at the end of the next class I gave the paper to him and to my surprise he glanced at it, said, "Great,' then asked when could we begin to meet. We agreed upon meeting after each class in his office. By this time, my interest was piqued. I wanted to see what God was going to do. This man did not know me yet and somehow was able to see me. I wanted to be guarded but the inner me wondered could this be the right time; will it happen now? I'd been praying for freedom but could not identify just what kept me feeling stifled at times.

I knew I needed help to unveil what seemed to keep blocking me? I was so good at so many things. I was by now more involved in my church working with all ages and people from all walks of life. I had grown in all areas, able to see God's hand at work in my life. Speaking and being used to minister to hundreds of souls, laying on of hands, feeling God's power work in me. I had experienced working abroad as a missionary teaching, which was rewarding and fulfilling.

Now I had come to a point where God was telling me, 'I can indeed use broken vessels. I specialize in that. Janet, it's time, I need YOU whole for the next phase of your assignment. I need for you to let me reach into the deep crevices of your soul and heal ALL your wounds. I can do it, I'm God, trust me once again I will not let you down.'

As I drove home that night contemplating the day and wondering what God was up to I remember driving, crying, and telling God, 'I try, what more do you want from me? I give you my best as much as I can.' To which the response came, 'I know you give me your best, you do, but I want your worst.'

I was of course baffled by this and it didn't seem to add any kind of consolation to what I was feeling. I felt myself exhale deeply as I whispered, 'I just don't understand.' At that moment it was as though Jesus became my personal storyteller, as I listened, I could visualize the whole scenario in my mind.

If you were to receive news that the king was coming to visit with you and would be eating with you, what would you do? Chances are you would first and foremost clean your house. You would dress your table with the finest of linen you could find. You would take out your best china and make sure everything was sparkling, simply because you want to honor him and present to him your very best. After all, this is the king. This all sounded quite logical to me and I didn't know what the lesson was in this visual illustration until I heard His voice say, "Janet you have given me your best all these years, now I need you to trust Me and give Me the parts of you that you see as your worst. You see, unlike an earthly king, I can and want to use all of you. You see that chipped cup in the closet I can use that too, that fork that has been bent from years of use I can use that too, the plate with the stain thrown in the back of the closet, you can bring it out. There is no need to hide them from Me any longer. You see I need all of you even the broken pieces even the rough places let Me walk in them. It's time!"

Wow! How indeed could I respond?

And so, I sat with Professor Sanders and we began, I can't even remember how or what we started with. He asked questions I responded. We talked about educational goals, or where I thought God was leading me. I do know that at one point the questions began to point towards my family. The roles we all seemed to have. Even as children, what were our roles? As we talked it became evident that we did have them.

Dawn, I talked about the name-calling you suffered, you know, the big eye toad bitch mum would call you. Do you remember that one? I do. I talked about you being my world. How I just wanted to be like you. To me, you could do everything, and no one could resist you. You didn't even have to try. You would be hard aloof, and it seemed tough people male or female would be drawn to you. There I was always in the shadow of you, but it was okay because to me even your shadow was great.

I don't remember how but one day after a few months of our sessions. He asked about how I felt when certain things happened that I would describe. The fights with mum and dad, the shouting, the fear as we would lay on the floor by the door and listen to the raised voices, the scuffled sounds of feet, the shoving, or the sound of pain in the form of anguished grunts, of the breaking glass, or things being thrown. Always mums voice louder, remember she would be screaming, 'Kill me... Kill me, you murderer.'

I just wanted them to have peace. I learned to be accommodating, always, to my detriment. Don't argue or fight, don't get angry because when people get angry, they argue, and then they fight, and then they will leave you. I also learned that whatever you do, don't hurt people. You can deal with your hurt but not the guilt of having hurt someone else.

During this time, I was struggling as to why I felt I kept going around in circles. I knew I was in Christ and whom the Son set free is free indeed, right. So why had I been feeling this sense of being blocked or held at a standstill? My lost love had long gone by now but still, it seemed the residue was there. It had been over nine years now and I was still cold. Constantly putting out the vibes that sent a very clear message of don't even look my way.

I felt as though I had been robbed yet again. What was someone going to tell me now that I hadn't already heard? Or promise me what already had been promised. So why bother I thought? I became known as the girl that was going to say no. So why ask? Or at least that was what I was told by people, and I owned it quite proudly. Silly right? Being proud of being locked in your prison. I had already been told that I was not enough. Do you remember that song mum would play the lyrics were? 'I'm nobody's child. I'm nobody's child. Just like a flower, I'm growing wild. No mummy's kisses and no daddy's smile. Nobody wants me I'm nobody's child.'

I wondered if that was her cry! Still there I was.

Professor Martin seemed intrigued about our relationship. As sisters, we didn't fight and had no sibling rivalry. How perfect you must have been, incredibly special to me. When you talked to me you would think that I only had one sister. In my mind there was only you after all we had grown up separated from two older siblings we knew very little about. Two girls, my mother had when she was in her late teens. She had left them as babies in another country to be cared for by their father's family. Hopey and Jennifer. Hopey, the eldest did come and stay with us for a short time when she was eleven years old, but it was not good. The trauma, the accusations she experienced from mom was too much and some four or five years later she was gone. Preferring to live with virtual strangers, she left that dark house. She left the country. Never to be seen again until I was an adult. I was only about five years old at that time and so it did feel as though it was just the three of us because it was.

Why did the topic of the games we used to play come up during the conversation? For the first time in my life, I heard my lips speaking the things that were so deeply locked away. When I said it out loud I felt guilty as though I had betrayed the trust we had. I had told the secret to someone else and there was no going back. These had been more than just games children played, beyond the boundary of doctor and nurse games. One evening Professor Sanders said to me that I needed to admit that there were elements that were unhealthy about our sisterhood. My heart began to pound again. What was he saying? Where was he going with this? What was he asking me to do? It was hard for me to even acknowledge what he was asking me to admit. I knew it was just something I didn't talk about, couldn't talk about, shouldn't talk about. I knew there was guilt and shame and I knew that I had felt that same thing when someone of the opposite sex would approach me. Even in my few relationships, I could detach from where I was if I was touched or kissed. I was uncomfortable being kissed. I would just go to my place outside of myself until it stopped. I just would not allow myself to feel.

Finally, Professor Sanders said, "Janet, I know that you love your sister, but she was wrong."

Wrong how? Could that be? I could push that stuff aside because look at how close we are to each other. Look at what God has done for us and how he kept us all those weeks, we would be home alone. The bills were paid, dad made sure of that but so many times there was no food to eat because dad had not come to the house for a week or sometimes more. There was no food for days, even when he came we wouldn't ask. You would always make me laugh to forget the hunger. Or we would trade in the soda bottles to get some chips and we were fine, and no one would know. I could say all of these things.

Professor Sanders looked at me intently and said, "Janet when you were a child you learned about sexual things, oral sex from your sister, she was wrong! A grown-up activity which was taught by your sister. That is not okay, and it is not normal. You have to admit that to yourself. It will not take anything away from you loving your sister. But wrong is wrong, she was wrong."

He went on to say, "Your family experience can easily distort what it means to love and have intimacy. You have allowed that to play out in other relationships. No one gets to you. You have shut down. You detach. You cannot be happy."

With a look of great concern and maybe sad empathy he leaned forward and asked the question, "Does your pastor know about your story?" I shook my head to which he responded, "How could he not know?"

Dawn, my dear sister, to hear it made my world crumble and God broke me right there as scene after scene played in my mind. What was I doing? Lying in our brother's room and letting even a cousin follow your every instruction to explore my private parts.

The guilt, the tears began to flood again, only it was different, I was shaking as the hero image I had of the only person that cared for me was shattered. It wasn't perfect, and that realization hurt. I told him to stop because you were all I had. My mother had left, my father was absent in every way. You took care of me. You watched out for me, you were my sister. I would have done anything for you not to leave me too. Not to hate me. Not to discount me. I told him that I could not think of you in another way because I felt that if you take the perfect picture of my protector away what would I have left. To me, it would then mean that I had nothing and never did.

When you live in dysfunction for so long it will be all you know and somewhere in the recesses of your inner self, you try to make it seem normal and even okay. Yet in the midst of it all you know it's not, your soul and your spirit tell you that something is not right. You close that door when it's too painful to comprehend and never open it. It's a door somewhere where you hope you will never have to see it again.

A normal family childhood? NO! I guess not for me, I didn't deserve that.

That was supposed to be one of the well-kept secrets. That's why this child had learned to smile on the outside while she crumbled on the inside. Yet there I was, and it was oozing out as if someone was slowly loosening the lid of a pressure cooker. With calm and steady expertise this professor skillfully opened the closet. Years of guilt and shame that just reinforced the idea that I was so unworthy so bound to stay in that dark place of secrecy to protect my distorted childhood and more importantly, to protect the hero in you, dear sister, the hero I needed you to be, at least in my world. As we went further and further it was clear that some spiritual strongholds were at work.

Soon I would come to learn that some of these spiritual strongholds were known as familiar spirits, generational strongholds that God was about to expose, uproot and destroy.

Food for Thought:

Sometimes you will find yourself in a place where you think you are there for one thing, but God has an entirely different plan. Sometimes all you want to do is find a place of peace where you can get away from the nagging whispers trying to keep you bound. A hiding place. You just want to get away to freedom. When the truth is, freedom is not away somewhere outside of you. True freedom must come from within. But the truth is when you ask God to take control, guide your life and lead your path be prepared to encounter yourself and all that's within on the way!

Prayer Point

Lord thank You for guiding my steps. Even when I try to hide from myself, Your love finds me, Your love draws me. Help me to remember that You see into the most inner core of me and that You hear the silent screams, you see the invisible tears.

Lord help me to trust that You will never expose me to humiliate me. I am in Your hand, I'm walking in the Master's plan. I am on my way to victory. I'm on my way to wholeness!

In the name of Jesus.

12

Chapter

DELIVERANCE! WHO ME?

*I*t wasn't long after these traumatic and very emotionally packed sessions that Professor Sanders asked me if I would be willing to talk to another couple. Dr. John Ellenberger and his wife, Helen. He had taken me as far as he felt he could go and suggested that I take the next step in my hunger for freedom and release. Now they were an elderly couple who both worked at the seminary. I knew them and knew that they were well known for their deliverance ministry. To their credit, they had over forty years of experience working in such countries as Africa, Hattie, and many other countries over the mission field. God had given them a powerful ministry. They were humble, quiet, and dearly loved among the campus community and beyond.

By this point, I just wanted to be free. I wanted to stop the cycle. I wanted to feel me. Approach the little girl in that locked room, just maybe bring her out into the light. I was scared at first, but each session with this professor would leave me more and more drained, yet more and more convinced that this was not where God intended me to stay. It was time to take responsibility for who I was and who I would become. My past did not have to equal my future and it needed to no longer cripple my present. How empowering that thought would become on this journey to freedom, wholeness, and spiritual health. I did not have to allow myself to be defined by my past.

I was determined that where I had been would not be allowed to determine where I was going. This was my journey and with God's help, I was going to take charge. I was willing to finally let go of anything and everything that could come between where I was and the relentless push, the hunger that said to me there is more waiting.

I felt it was like standing on the edge of a cliff with my eyes closed and letting go. I would have to be willing to fall, be vulnerable and let God catch me. To truly trust God as he had asked me to so many times. I had presented my best to God and he was saying to me, now give me your worst. Let me take the parts of you that hurt, that are broken, that you hide from all others, which no eyes can see. Give me the wounds, the weights you have been carrying, give me your strength, and give me the stench of your sinful past. I already freed you, the day you asked me to come into your life, I did, to make you a new person. You are new believe that wholeheartedly my child. You don't begin deep cleaning a house before you have purchased it and moved in to dwell in it. I'm house cleaning and all I ask now is that you allow me to reach into the crevices of your being. I already set you free, let me heal you.

What a revelation that was to me. To be free and still not healed yet made so much sense. That was it, that was what seemed to stand in my path and caused this tug of war at times. I needed complete healing. It was great that I had come to know Jesus in a personal way, however, He does not ask us to throw away who we are to come to Him. He says come as you are and then He causes us to see who we can be. Allowing us to reset our lives and make the choice to choose His path.

In this place, grace and mercy were meeting me once again and showing me there was another level of anointing, a broader field of ministry. God was not interested in me trying to impress Him by all the things I could do in service within the church. After all, He already knew what He had placed within me. With all the committees or evangelistic teams, all the preaching, the singing, the teaching, I was still the classic wounded healer and now the Master Physician had stepped in and was saying it was my turn. Yes, God uses broken vessels,

A broken spirit and contrite heart he will not despise. (Psalms 51:17) But He doesn't leave them that way, Praise God! and because He is the master potter in life's ever-turning wheel, He can take that marred vessel into the potter's house and His skillful hands. He will, because He loves us and will break us if He must, to make us over, a new vessel one that is whole without cracks. God knows a cracked vessel will only leak and become weak. Like cracked glass, it will not be able to stand under pressure and whatever is poured in it will soon be lost. I did not want to be a leaking vessel.

God was about to make an incredibly special deposit into my vessel, only He needed to prepare it, He needed me whole. When God brings you to the brink of a new horizon, you know it. You may not be able to tell just what it will look like on the other side but if you trust Him you will receive a confirmation deep down in your soul that you are almost there and that it is time to cross.

My life experience had taught me a cruel lesson, that everyone that said they loved me left. Mum said it, but she was gone by the time I was nine years old. Dad never said it. Come to think of it I can't think of how he showed it, I just assumed he must, but I was never sure. Dawn, I felt your protection for me was how you loved me even if you never said it.

Then there came the time when you to had to leave, to cleave to your husband and even that wasn't happening as long as I was around. I knew I had to leave and go far. God set it up that way I believe. Do you remember me asking you if it was okay for me to leave? I think part of me wanted to know that you would be okay without me. Neither one of us had let too many people get close to us. We were so connected, inseparable, more than each other's best friend. It was the kind of connection people say you find with identical twins, the kind where little to nothing needs to be said to send a message or felt across hundreds of miles. We both experienced that so many times I know. But also, I think I still needed to know I could now be without you. It was going to be my turn to learn what my name sounded like, to stand alone, hear my voice, and find out who I am.

So, I came to the States. I was a cautious twenty-two-year-old. Then comes this man, he says he loves me, clings to me one moment, and is gone the next. It was close to ten years later and I knew that I was not free from the effects and fear that had developed in my life of being left, pushed away, and discounted. I was fighting the sense of both physical and emotional abandonment. Do you remember I used to keep asking you when I was little? Do you love me, Dawn? I didn't realize that little girl was so lost, so insecure. So, trapped by the person she allowed everyone else to tell her she was or by what she felt circumstances had continually confirmed.

I did go to see the Ellenberger's. My first session was spent talking about what they saw as the spiritual issues. They had talked with my professor and seemed to understand more than I did what had been taking place. Outside of these three people I had told no one about what was going on at that time. No one knew about this war that was raging within me, no one knew of these family secrets. Let's see, just how I was supposed to explain this crossroad. I wasn't ready to have to answer anyone's questions about our childhood or to hear the disapproving, condemning, or judgmental responses.

How was I going to be able to reveal it all and still protect you at the same time? When I had spoken to Professor Martin and confessed for the first time in my life those things which had happened, I felt a guilt that said

I had betrayed you and our secret shame. Like right now writing this, I must risk the chance of hurting you to be able to save you, and me. To bring us to the place of total freedom and healing, I see the possibilities, I taste the freedom. I know I MUST do this and there is a sense of urgency that I can't explain to do this NOW!

Again, I was asked does your pastor know what you have been through and where you are now. When I said no, they were astounded. How could he not know when you are part of the leadership team? The answer was quite simple really; I didn't tell him. Even within the church, there seemed to be an unspoken culture of things that were not talked about, could not be shared. Not if you were really saved. So, I didn't talk about myself to others and I didn't feel safe. It's sad to say but true, I had not gone to those dark places until now. I listened to others, I helped others and I focused on the needs of others. I could sense and have genuine empathy for those who were hurt or hurting. I could feel their need before they opened their mouths at times. Even in my situation, God was able to use this broken vessel to bless others, encourage others and pull others out of their dark place. The more He used me, the humbler I felt, for I knew it was only by His mercy and His grace.

During our first meeting, they gave me some homework. They told me what they were going to do but before they would begin. They needed me to go home and reflect, and just write down everything I could think of. Which was to include everything that had crept into my life, that was not of God whether it was something I did, was involved in, or had been done to me, even things I was not responsible for but had felt the effects of.

The life-changing instruction given was to remember the pain of the moment and to call it for what it was. Not to use any watered-down names for the acts but to speak out the truth, face the sound of hearing the words. What happened, what was done, what residue or feelings resulted, and then renounce it. If it was shame, then what was the thing that first caused me to feel shame? Recall it, say it, remember it, renounce it and then ask

God to reclaim his place there. This is an immensely powerful thing my sister, one you need to do if you have not done so, in those four deliberate steps recall, remember, renounce, and reclaim.

I wrote them down, did as they asked, and then went back. There were three people there and they explained to me that they were going to talk to the very issues that had been operating in and around my life. My role was to let whatever wanted to come out come out, not to sensor the thoughts, responses, or what I heard in my mind's ear. The instructions were that as I heard them speak, I should not try to control them or silence them. Not to protect the whispering or the lies I would hear.

One person would speak, Dr. Ellenberger, while his wife was going to be in continual intercession. The third person recorded what took place. It almost sounded like a scene out of some horror or suspense movie, but I am not crazy this was all too real, and more than that I was right there in the midst. I wasn't watching a movie, it was me. I was so nervous, but I wanted so desperately to be released, to be able to let go and not have the lingering feelings of shame guilt, and secrecy. I didn't want to be locked in that dark place within anymore. It was time to be braver than I had ever thought I could be, at least for myself. It had been easy to fight for others, but now I would have to fight for myself. I would have to dare to open that door fully.

Dear sister, you once said that you felt that there were some things passed down to us from birth, generational things, well I found out that you were right, I heard them!

Food for Thought

Someone once said the only way to know where your going is to know where you have been. The Journey forward into freedom and! wholeness may take you to a place in the past long forgotten. To walk in wholeness, we must be willing to deal with the leaky holes of our sometimes-fractured inner child. Having the courage to take off the mask. It is okay to be fed up with telling people it's okay when it really isn't. God knows every corner of shame, closet of guilt, residue of pain, embers of hope and longing. If you listen, you will hear him as he beckons, "Take off your mask. Let me love the darkness you hide underneath, and it will turn to light. I still create diamonds while they are yet covered by dirt.

Prayer Point

Lord, I admit that there are issues in my life that are beyond me. I admit that it is sometimes easier to hide the truth of my struggles and to put on a good face. [A mask] I need Your help. Lord, send someone to meet me on this journey who will be Your hand and Your voice of truth and hope.

Amen.

13

Chapter

REMEMBER, RENOUNCE, RECLAIM, RELEASE, RENEW

I did what they asked me to do and prepared to meet them once again. After praying and asking if I was ready, we began. I didn't know what was going to take place or what this journey would be like. I just believed that whatever was going to happen it would take me to a better place. A place of freedom where there was going to be peace and I would be able to help you, my dear sister, to get there too.

Dr. Ellenberger would call out loud the name of the very thing I wrote down. The questions would be asked, "Who are you? How did you gain access? And what gives you the right to continue to operate in her life?

I never realized that there could be doorways for spiritual interference to enter your life, did not know that others could bring them or introduce them into your life, especially if you are a child. I want to share with you briefly what I learned that night.

Lust said, 'I began when she was four years old the door was opened and never shut I have the right to be here because no one addresses me.

Aloneness, not loneliness, said, 'I have always been here from her mother, her grandmother, look at the women in her family, I have worked, they ended up alone. I mess things up. I must isolate her I serve Me, I and Myself.' When asked what gave him the right to continue to operate in my life, the reply was, 'Because it is so. It is the truth and my mark is on her. She is alone, I've got her.'

Suddenly Fear raised his head but did not speak it was the silent invisible chain holding all the others in place.

Shame said, 'I am here to remind her of the past, I remind her she was there, but I can only work with those things she has kept as secrets. I serve Me!'

Guilt said, 'I am a friend to shame and we have a right because of lust's secrets. We have made sure she can not get away from what she has done, what we saw.'

If I said that I was a child and did not have control. Shame would say quickly, 'If she thinks of opening that door remind her she can't trust these men, she will get hurt. We tell her, Oh, if someone were to find out. We bring the pictures to her mind, we make her see where she has been and tell her to stay in the dark little girl, behave, be silent, don't come out stay in the dark where it is safe, and they can't see us, that way you won't get hurt.

Death said, 'Go away it's none of your business, she's lost, she went away when she was five. What had left was the sense of innocence, pure unmarred, unstained innocence. I am only here to kill her; she must not live. I have the right to operate because of fear. She is weak and I know the secret.'

Nothing said, 'I am the name of the little girl. I have the right because she believes she is nothing and she is weak. She fears her sister. No one listens to her, she has no voice of her own. I call her nothing because she is nothing. She sits and cries in the dark, she closes the door, she does not speak that little girl has no name, she is nothing. There is no need for more. I remind her that she is in the shadow in the dark. No one wants her.'

There was one identifying itself as the bitch. It said, 'I keep the little girl in check, I protect her. Stand between them and her. I don't care. I will do it and I'll show you; you can't get me. You can touch me, but you can't get me. I take her to the wrong places; she uses me to try and be tough. Do you want to know how many of us there are? Count them yourself.'

Again, fear came forward. This time he answers the questions. 'I came when it all began, the touching. I serve that I cannot tell, he's dark. My job is to make her remember, secrets and hurts. She does not like me. I have the right to stay because she's afraid of losing those around her, she's afraid to love, afraid to die, to hurt. No big deal I have been here for generations from her grandfather.'

Finally, the most stubborn of all was that of lies: Who said, 'It is my job to persuade her, to deceive and make room for the others to work.'

Dawn, these spirits spoke. I heard them like an out-of-body experience, but I was right there. I heard the words in my head come out of my mouth. I felt as though I was in a crowd and had been pushed into the background. One by one they were commanded to return to the pit of hell. As we went through the process of renouncing and reclaiming, I had to open my mouth and say spirit of shame you no longer have the right to operate in my life. I renounce you. For each one, I had to open MY mouth speaking these words with a new power. It was a long night, but I was not alone, there were three spiritual giant warriors constantly praying and interceding. Dr. Ellenberger lead me though while his wife never spoke but never stopped interceding on my behalf, while the other gentleman prayed for the elderly couple leading the way into this spiritual battlefield, fully armed with the weapons of spiritual warfare. It was a battlefield of the mind for a release of the soul.

I remember at one point being on the ground. It was time for the little girl to unlock the door and come out. I could not, I was afraid, fear was whispering in my ears. But they compelled, and I was desperate for the inner struggle to cease. I could feel the little girl inside named, 'Nothing,' wanting to lift her head and look up, to unlock the door and walk out of her own prison. To get out of the fetal position, the one I was now physically, emotionally, and spiritually in. I had to push, I had to press. I kept waiting for the rescue, for the walls of that dark closet to crumble and set me free.

As she dared to lift her head, the feeling in the room became more intense. It was time, finally, death had to loosen its grip, fear had to back off.

Dawn, I saw the door of that dark room open and light filled the doorway. A blinding light so breathtakingly bright beyond any I have ever seen before or could adequately explain with words. All I know is there was a figure and I knew it was Jesus. I thought He was going to rush in to scoop me up and take me out of this place but that did not happen. His hand reached for me, but He did not move. Why wasn't He coming for me, couldn't He see what I had been through, was going through right now. He remained still and His arms were outstretched. I could not see Him, but I could feel His expression was one of peace. He was not worried. Then I got it. I was still in the corner of that room. I would have to trust Him, I had to reach out to him. He would not force me, I was the one that needed to go to Him.

"And ye shall seek me and find me when ye shall search for me with all your heart." (Jeremiah 29:13)

All I can tell you is that as that little girl reached out and touched that outstretched hand, something unexplainable happened. That light traveling like a flash of lightning rushed in and consumed every corner of that room. That little girl stood and walked right into the bright light. I didn't realize at first, although this was all going on in the spirit that I had physically lifted my hands and was reaching out. I felt the warmth of His touch fill my very being, every limb, every vein receiving His light. Inside I feel the warmth. I feel as though I am floating, lifted into the light. Then I hear a voice say, "Your name is no longer 'Nothing,' but I give you a new name and it shall be LIFE and GLORY!"

By now I am uncontrollably sobbing, my breathing was different and overall relief was consuming my body. As these dear seasoned warriors of God continued to gently yet unwaveringly. Under God's guide, they would uncover the residue of generational secret familiar spirits then gently yet with all authority covered me in prayer.

LIFE and GLORY HALLELUJAH! I had a new name. Like Jacob, I had wrestled and refused to let go until freedom and wholeness came until Jesus came! I would show forth the Glory of God and live! I wept, as I began to praise God right there. He had rescued me from a past I had no power over and was sealing me for a future He had destined.

I was overwhelmed by everything knowing I was now truly free. I found myself wondering what it all meant and how I was going to explain this. I was not possessed but so many areas of my life would keep coming to a roadblock or, I would find myself continually struggling in a particular area. I would know that there was more for me but not be able to press for it. Now God was taking me to another level of awareness and ministry. He had already told me that He needed me to be whole.

Remember the story of the little boy who found out that Jesus was coming to His house, so he prepared as best he could. When Jesus arrived, he began to move about the house from room to room, in the kitchen, bathroom, up the stairs all over. The little boy was so excited Jesus had chosen to come to his house. Suddenly without a word, the boy sees Jesus turn and begin to leave. The boy tries to stop Him. "Jesus, why are You leaving, what can I do? please don't go. Everything I have is Yours."

Finally, Jesus asks, "What about that small closet at the top of the stairs? Why is it locked?"

Somewhat taken back the boy responds, "Oh that's nothing Jesus, just a tiny closet. I keep a few things locked in there. It's not important. It's just some very private things, old and dusty. But everything else is wide open Lord." The boy is surprised as Jesus continues to leave.

"Jesus wait why are you going?" the boy questions. Jesus turns and says softly, "If I cannot be Lord of ALL, I can not be Lord at all."

He had been with me in my house and now I was opening that private closet I had kept locked, even from myself. The secrets of the past could no longer hold me captive. There were to be no more ghosts allowed to hide. No more dark closets.

I had to say all this because it was then that God told me that I was delivered but for my complete healing I must now release the secret, I have to talk to my sister. We both have to take off the mask and let down the veil, God needed to heal her too. God told me that all is not what it seems with my sister, she needed me, but not as her baby sister. She needs what God had deposited in me. God wants to release her and release her gifts too.

Dawn, I can't express how much I struggled with it. I didn't know how to bring these things up. That must have been in early November. I took all the notes that Dr. Ellenberger had because I wanted to be able to read it and know for myself the details of that night. That's how I can tell you some of what was said and done that night. The above account is taken right out of those notes I still have.

I also began to learn from them the steps to this model of deliverance. The insight they gave has been invaluable which rests on the authority of God himself.

The authority He gives us to put the enemy of our souls under our feet.

Food for Thought

God is ever-present and like a father, He will NOT allow those who put their trust in Him, those who are surrendered to Him, those who call out to Him to be overwhelmed. God's love is greater than the darkness you find yourself going through.

Prayer Point

Lord when my heart is overwhelmed, I will run to the rock that is higher than I. I will call upon the Lord who is worthy to be praised so I shall be saved from my enemies. In my distress I can call, I can cry out to You, Lord. You hear my voice from Your temple. Your bow the heavens, You will come down riding upon a cherub. As You thunder from heaven You will send out arrows. You will take me and draw me out of the waters. The Lord delivered me from my strong enemy and from them that hated me because they were too great for me. God, I thank You that you are able to release us from the past, to change what we see in the present and to give us a new name for the future. I declare that I will no longer be bound! You are my victory.

Thank You, my God, for rescuing me!
—*Psalm 144:5*

14

Chapter

SHE'S GONE!

Then in December mum was so insistent that I join her in Jamaica for a vacation. I was not interested at all, reluctantly, both I and my dear friend Doreen decided to go. This again would prove to be a divine appointment by God's design, for He knew what was about to happen. I had even taken the notes from my time with the Ellenberger's with me to analyze. Not knowing much about Jamaica or any of mum's family there, I thought maybe I can do some research while there and find answers. That's how fresh this all was. I was going to talk to mum, but I never got the chance to. Six days after arriving in Jamaica, on Christmas Day, mum would have a massive stroke. Ten days after that I would bury her there, I was still in a daze.

I need to confess that I was angry at all of my family. Angry that I was there in this strange land that I knew nothing about. No one could come to be with us, even when mum first had the stroke. I cared for her alone with Doreen. There are so many unpleasant details of this trip I have chosen not to go into here. The baby of the family had somehow become the caregiver. Everyone looking at me and asking me what to do. She died alone still loving a man who did not want her. I remember looking deep into her eyes, it all seemed so unfair.

As I looked into her, I saw her tired soul and broken heart and it hurt so much. I wasn't finished with her yet. I wanted to do so much for her. During her last two years, having surrendered her life to Christ, she was doing so well. She had become such a loving woman, sold out to God, and wanted nothing more than her husband and family. I wanted to find out about this family I had come from but that was not to be.

I wondered what God could be doing. If I had just been freed from the past and all the abandonment why would He then take her now? Why now when I needed her? I even tried to find my darkroom and that little girl so I could run to the darkness once again to hide from the cruelty of this moment, it had always been so familiar to me. The place I had always gone to, where I could hide and not feel.

The funny thing is I couldn't find it. I had forgotten in that moment of grief it was no longer there. But I did have the light of life and the power of God's Glory that was going to keep me and give me supernatural strength.

I did find that one of our cousins had been dabbling with spiritualist people and going to them. Some woman she said was helping her get rid of a hex. This cousin told me a few days before mum's stroke of one of her recent visits. I cannot tell you of it right now. But it sounded strange to me. Not Godly at all. Dawn, when we next meet, we will talk. Right now, God wants to release us and finally break the bonds that have bound us. Everything that the devil meant to destroy us God is using to build us.

There is so much more. It all had a purpose. I never dreamt that He would take her just then in the midst of all this. Not after all I had just been through. There was so much I had wanted to do for her. God had been good and answered our ten-year prayer to save her. He did and what a transformation. Finally!

Yet there I was watching her, searching her face, looking into her soul in that hospital as if to burn the image of her face deep in my memory bank. I sang to her, read scriptures to her, fed her, cleaned her. I never let her see me cry. Outside the ward, I would fall against the wall and sob after I had left her there. They didn't care for her right. I wanted to take her home, but they wouldn't let me. They said if I moved her, she would not make it.

There I was not knowing anyone or anything about Jamaica and I was alone but not on my own, Doreen was so faithful in trying to watch over me. Over the years mum had come to love her like a daughter. It was fitting that she would be there. She was a rock. Still, I could not help thinking where was my family? Why wouldn't my siblings come and help me? Tell me what to do.

On one of my visits, Mum talked about my children she hadn't seen yet. The unborn grandchildren she often imagined and longed to one day to see.

She reached her weakened hand out and rested it on the small of my back. She knew I was tired. She knew I was there alone but seemed thankful that Doreen was there with me. Mum knew I was no match for the people there. Though the culture was a part of my makeup I knew very little about the people. I remember when she gave me her wedding bands and just said take care of yourself baby. Of course, I told her to stop, but I saw in her eyes. Those eyes I spent all those hours looking so intently in. She was tired too. Don't worry she said I know where I'm going. I wanted to stop her Dawn. Tell her not to leave me yet.

I tried to get her back, but I couldn't. Again, it was my fault I felt. I should have pressed harder. I still see her eyes. But I am so grateful she has no more pain. I asked God not to let her suffer and He heard that prayer. Isn't it funny, she would die before she would get one of her greatest wishes, to have all her family together? We had never all been together.

My sister, do not become weary in well-doing. Do not give up on your marriage until you hear and know God says to. There is too much at stake. You have already been through and seen too much. You were searching too. You have been alone too, even in marriage. But you had to be the responsible one.

Dawn, know that this same mother who could so easily scorn you as a child, had to turn around and call you blessed. Blessed you are because you did not let those things turn you against her.

This has been a lot to take in and please know that it is not written for you to feel guilty. But I am in a desperate place. I have wasted so many years wanting to finally be something to someone. I think that this season was for me to understand that I couldn't have found that. How could I finally mean something to someone when I was struggling not to be a nothing to myself?

I began this by saying some things would be hard to read or receive but that I needed to be free to not just be delivered but to continue in wholeness. This is the right time, I feel the urgency, we both need this I know it. I am willing to count the cost.

Sometime later there I was, I had met someone who seemed to look right into my soul. Always watching me looking into me. I still had those old barriers up but he seemed to search for my heart. He reached it, held it but wouldn't cover it. I had allowed this person to put me through so much. When In the past I would have shut off. I found I could not this time. I couldn't detach or pretend. We grew close, he would push away and then pull me in, too many times. One day he told me that my love gets in the way of us growing, I was speechless. I think I stopped breathing for a few moments. I threw my hands and my heart up, I loved him but I was so beaten and so I let go, stepped back. The pain of that moment, those days was so very unbearable. You know. I would sob on the way to work. Contain with all my might, fight back the tears, and then at break run to find a place to let it out again. How could he not know, not see, not believe?

My translation was that my love was an inconvenience that got in the way. Talk about a kick in the gut.

I was reminded and understood that I needed to be changed. The pain in my inner being at the idea of not loving and not being with him reminded me. I was crushed as I backed away with no heart, just dust. Then here we go again. I found myself searching for my darkroom to go and hide in, the once safe place. That was when I would tell you that I didn't want to die because I knew that if I found that place, I would lock me away. It had taken fifteen years since that, 'Dear John letter,' to feel from my heart again. I was afraid that if I went back to that room where the little girl had been locked away that it would be for good. Yet, in desperation, I tried to find it, but I couldn't. I couldn't thank GOD, I couldn't. It was still gone. Remember LIFE and GLORY! In all of this when I would try to run God would remind me of His purpose for my life. So regardless of how things felt or appeared He did have a purpose in all of this.

So, I ran to the source. I know that what God has for me cannot be mine until I am ready. Whether it would include him or anyone. God knows the heart within me. And yes, the hope.

As I fasted and prayed those seven days God was again peeling and reminding me. On the day I picked to pray about my family, I thought that I would be praying about my husband and my children and all that would come with them, you know future stuff. But instead, I found that I kept coming back to you dear sister, and me. During my break, down at the park, I was sitting alone reading and praying. Suddenly the pictures kept coming and the tears flowed. I had not completed my assignment those eight years ago. I knew just as I had experienced God's healing mercies, I was supposed to come to you then. I never came to you. I still hadn't broken the silence. It became so clear that if I was truly going to keep living in this wholeness, I needed to complete my assignment, my heart needed this, my soul needed this. You needed this. I had to text you.

I couldn't call because I think I would have chickened out. I would not have known what to say.

Even after I sent the text to let you know I had something important to write to you I was not sure of what your response would be. An hour later I read your response and thought finally Lord, no more ghosts, no more silence.

Well, there it is Dawn as condensed as I can make it. We have all done things we are not proud of. Thank God for mercy and grace and His love that is able to cover a multitude of sins. I don't want to live my life how others view me. I don't want to live according to their perceptions anymore. I am learning while man may give you an identity by how they view you, treat you, speak to you, and respond to you, or even what they may call you; God is not concerned or deterred by your identity. His Word says that He has made man to be in His image. His gift to me is not an identity but His image. One by which when others see me when I look at myself, I can reflect the Glory of God. It is my purpose and His will for me. Love is truly powerful. I asked for change, I asked for a transformation. I asked for a God thing and He's doing it.

My Life for His Glory.

So, if God must tear up the identity I was given to make me over in His image then so be it. I want Jesus and ALL that He has for me. So, I don't know about tomorrow, but I know that there is within me a love that I have not encountered before waiting to find a resting place, the right place for God to release it all. A love that has caused me to face myself and put down everything, no masks. Jesus goes before me and I know that if tomorrow I can stay close to the one who does all things well, it will be alright.

So much more to share but it will have to wait. The purpose of this chapter is complete.

A Journey from Wellness to Wholeness
October 24th, 2006

I have just finished reading this for myself. I have wept, held myself, remembered, and wondered how I got through writing it, pondered if I should change it. Prayed and today October 24th I am releasing it ALL into GOD'S care. Thank you, Jesus.

Food for Thought

What giants, what secrets are you willing to face for you to gain compete victory. Sometimes in order to move forward, you must be willing to go back.

To gain what you need; you must first be willing to lose the thing you want, let go of what is in your hand. Is there a friend, a family member, a relationship that you need to take an honest look at? Are there dysfunctions, unhealthy alliances that need to be released? We desperately hold on at times, afraid to let go and give God something. Even while it means we will gain everything. Many people find themselves willing to protect the very thing or person that has caused them pain for fear of hurting someone else's feelings. Having to figure out how to live life without them can be scary. My dear friend this is YOUR time. Do not remain bound to the things that eat away at your present.

It is the truth that will set you free. So be courageous enough to face the giant whatever it is and know that the Father will not let it consume you.

Prayer Point

Lord, I am ready to be whole. Still, there are times I want to wither away from the things that arise and make me uncomfortable. Sometimes I find that I seem more concerned about how others might perceive me. I am not always strong enough to say what needs to be said, I do not always have my voice. Whispers in my mind about my self-worth echo from behind that locked door telling me to hide. I am tired of wearing a mask and worrying about what others will think. I hear you calling me, leading me into freedom. I am ready to walk, to face what lies behind that secret closet door of my soul...

I choose wholeness, I choose freedom, I choose life, I choose You and I choose me. For whom the Son sets free, is free indeed. Like David, I declare that THIS DAY as I come in the name of the Lord I will stand! I shall not wither into the background of my past. I will live and declare the works of the Lord to the Glory of God! Let's go!!

15

Chapter

AND THEN IT CAME

Today is November 26ᵗʰ, 2006 at 6:27 p.m.

And so here I am ready to continue this journey from wellness to wholeness. I had been fasting for seven days. No food, only vitamin water, and bottled water to sustain me. Something told me that I was going to need God's divine strength, wisdom, and fortitude.

There would be moments when my heart would be racing wondering what Dawn was thinking. I knew it would take a few days for her to receive it in England. I counted the days for this was no ordinary note and I believe I felt the moment she had received it in her hands, said a prayer, and waited. I could see her in my mind's eye. The package was weighty, so I knew she would feel as she held it that it was important and that she would need a quiet place alone. I wasn't sure what would happen once she had read it, but I knew this was God's time and it was now completely in His hands.

Healing was on the way and I was still yearning for that promised strength to keep walking in the new freedom. I could feel it bursting to erupt in my soul and I knew this phase was part of the key to my breakthrough.

I was surprised that it only took another one week for the reply to come. When it did, I was not prepared for what it would do or how it would come.

On the 8th of November, my fast was over and I met with three other ladies who had joined me on this week-long journey. Each day we would pray for a different aspect of life and spiritual living. We had agreed that this week we would lift each other up, touch and agree on behalf of our deepest needs, desires, and God's direction. That night we prayed realizing that though the fasting of food was over we were just about to see manifested in the visible what God had been doing all week long in the invisible. We may have all had different needs but that didn't matter, the mere strength and biblical principle of touching and agreeing were at work.

Thursday morning 9th November, I am in my classroom. For some reason I keep hearing the phone beep, there's a text message waiting for me. I was busy and didn't have time to look. At about 11 a.m. for some reason, the sound came back to my ear and I knew this time it was important for me to look at this message. I could feel it, it was time, it really was.

I asked for a break and found a quiet area in the backroom then opened the text. There it was a message from Dawn. What was it going to say? What was going to happen? What would she tell me now? As I read the words burned into my soul and the doors began to open to a place I could no longer contain. I could barely believe it as I began to read.

"Dear sister, you may not believe this but everything you have written down including the events at Nyack college God had shown me when I was visiting you this year in America. He also brought me back to my childhood and showed me the emotional abuse I had also gone through. He told me to write everything down and I did. I did not show you because He said he wanted to heal ME!

The pain that came was intense because I had also suppressed memories and shut down feelings. There is no more guilt or fear. God has taken it all and He told me never to pick it up again.

Yes, I too remember the goodnight kisses. Yes, Janet, it was not just you," she wrote.

I must confess that as I read those lines, 'It was not just you,' I broke down. All of this time, all of these many years, both of us hiding, keeping quiet, not talking. Right there in that back room in the middle of the day, the secrets, the ghosts began to be released, even more, healing had begun to flow.

I held my mouth as the tears began to stream down my face right there. Then I continued to read almost afraid of what it might reveal but needing to know. She continued.

"I would tell myself dad was just playing and then his hand would slip. It was all unintentional on his part. I had told myself to forgive and let go.

As for us siblings, we were wrong, young but wrong! We were unaware of the effects of childhood on adult life. The enemy can no longer hold you or me captive Janet. I am free. That was the ghost in my closet. I've kicked the door down. I am today no longer bound by the past as an eight-year-old girl who felt hated by her mother.

God's presence, His spirit washed over me just as I finished reading your journal/your letter, overwhelming me, I felt such pain oozing and brokenness being healed. I heard the Spirit say, 'I have plans for you my daughter, deliverance has come, get out spirit of lust, loneliness, and fear. I name you, now get out!"

On and on I read, eyes wide open trying to see through the tears that poured and attempted to blind my vision.

Her words went on to tell an account of then being caught up in a dream trance where she encounters personal spiritual surgery.

"My darling little sister, a nurse begins to take something out of my right arm with a needle. It was like a large snail when she got it out. It was scary to see, even scarier to imagine that it was coming from me. In this dream-like vision, the snail turned, looked at me, and lunged as if to attack me but it was blocked and could not touch me. Suddenly all at once, it vanished. I tell you little sister we are free!"

By the time I got to the end of the text tears were overflowing, and the intense emotions were overwhelming. I had to leave the room quickly, though I had been reading and oozing quietly so as not to draw attention to myself. I could feel this kind of intensity was not going to keep silent I could hear the sound of my pain pushing its way to the surface. As I rushed out into the hallway heading for the bathroom Karen one of the ladies that had been fasting with me stopped me. I could not speak. I handed her my phone to read and she read it, she began to smile.

A few days after I had mailed the letter to Dawn, I was so nervous that I had done it. So, I had given a copy of it to this trusted friend almost as a tester. What would I see in her eyes after she had come to know these things about me? I thought maybe I would have to get used to her now looking at me with disgust or pity. Instead, she came alongside me wanting to know how she could help, committed to walking with me through this journey. And so there she was standing in the hallway smiling this triumphant smile, "This is good isn't it? Look at God! This is awesome," she said. I was nodding, agreeing but it was all too much. I ran past her and headed straight to the bathroom. Thereafter locking the door I paced round and round, the words from her message rolling over and over in my head. I kept thinking, I did not know, I didn't know. Just to think of the years, the weight, the baggage, the burden, the isolation, and the chains that had bound us both for so long.

It is amazing what children will do or keep in the name of protecting each other. No wonder we clung to each other. We were inseparable. Not only did we cling to each other, but we kept everyone else out. Couldn't let them too close, we were afraid to let them see all the wounds that were seeping, the scars we were hiding. Keeping others at a distance was our safety net. You would have to be close to notice behind the smiles, the scars, or the wounds. No one ever made it until now. I can remember the pain oozing, then pouring, barely giving me room to breathe. I was down on the floor in the teacher's bathroom gasping to catch my breath, I began to hold onto the toilet bowl.

Here it was, we were both being set free; any lingering chains were falling and the weight being lifted. I wouldn't have to carry the secret anymore, to protect her. I could open my mouth I could speak out loud, I wouldn't have to pretend the memories were not real or not there. As I held onto that bowl now sobbing, finally letting go and giving way to the sound of my groans, it seemed as though everything began to gush out.

Outside the door I could hear Karen pacing back and forth praising God, raising her voice, not shouting but just enough for me to hear and know that I was not alone. She was encouraging me to let it all pour out, to take hold of the healing and embrace the new that God was pouring into my soul. I was not alone.

It felt as though I was a baby being born again. The tears were painful almost unbearable, but I knew they were good, they were needed, this was another level of healing and walking in the release I had been given. They were cleansing, purifying. They were what I had prayed for. It was the change, the release, the healing and transforming of the old into the new, and not for me only. I had told God that whatever it was this thing that I could not see, could not name but somehow seemed to block my path, whatever it was going to take to not be in that place I was willing to go through it. I asked God to show me, to do it. That is just what He was doing on that bathroom floor, stripping my very identity to reveal HIS image in me. I had found freedom, but I was still carrying my sisters' pain, carrying the burden of not having shared with her when I first encountered the release from that dark room.

I began to praise Him in the midst of the pain and how astounding the continual flow of the release that was taking place right there. It was powerful, enriching, and overwhelming all at once.

Food for Thought:

Sometimes it can be scary to take the steps you need to. As God leads you in walking out your transformation, you will soon find that it wasn't just about you. Your release can reach out to others and give them the courage to walk their own path to wholeness. You are connected, we are connected, we hold each other. The secret pain as it resides hidden will only compound the struggle to walk contrary to the effects of that pain. No man is an Island, and even when you try to live that way, you will find we are all still connected by the oceans of inner human complexities, emotions feelings, and experiences that flow between us. So be brave, be courageous in this hour, stand tall in His strength and step out into your complete release. Wholeness is available not just for you but for us!

Prayer Point

Lord though I am nervous to speak, nervous to release, I will trust You. For You have promised to be my strength when I am weak. You have walked with me, You have carried me, You will not leave me when I cry out to You. Just when I think I am on my own You will send the right word, the right friend to help me stand. Oh, how faithful is our God! Amen!

16
Chapter

FREEDOM

At that moment right there my phone rang, it was Dawn...as soon as I answered I heard her voice. "Hello baby sister, it's ok, it's alright we are finally free now." As soon as I heard her, my arms, my body went weak. Like so many times in my life without me saying anything she could feel me, she knew I needed her and my big sister came to cover me, to be sure that I was going to be alright. At that moment I felt what I will describe as a warm blanket of God's love wrap itself around us both. To shelter us under the shadow of His wings. We were the wounded healers and understood each other's spirit.

There she was, I was so happy I could hear her voice on the other end of that phone. Though we were separated by thousands of miles, I don't believe we had ever been closer than in that moment. God was taking all that the enemy had meant to kill us, divide us and He was giving us renewed life in Him with an even stronger bond and determination to follow after God.

He had been watching over us all the time. He had been preparing us all these years for this moment in time. The season was right, He had told me, it was time for a new anointing for a changed position and it would require a vessel with no blockages. He had not just saved me in the present to secure my future, but He was preparing me to be healed from my past and place me in a position to excel in the future.

Praise God! What a mighty God we serve. Could this all have been done years ago? Maybe so but I don't know if you can bring to God that which you do not see.

So, this was the right time, I had come to a place where my prayer included asking God to shine the light into any dark places and locked closets of my soul, I had to want it bad enough to open every part of my being, hand Him every hurt, every oozing wound. I would have to face the parts of me I didn't want to see, allow God to do it His way.

To let God lead me to that locked closet, to be willing to trust Him, reach for Him in and through the pain, to be able to face what He would have to show me hidden in that closet.

I had heard the inner whispers for years but was able to ignore them. They had become like the whispering sound of the wind, always present yet you can almost forget it's there because most of the time it is silent. Except every now and then you feel the chill of its touch as it brushes against your soul.

The door was opened, I had to look inside, I had to see, I could no longer ignore, I had to bring it all to God and release it into His hands. I had to ask Him to show me how to be changed. What was in the closet was not the image I saw written in His word.

After fifteen years of being emotionally closed to a relationship. I had let love in and be broken to the point of no freedom without release. However, I now knew what it was to love beyond my darkness, beyond the locked door, above my need to hide my shame or guilt. I loved beyond myself, above all I had ever known of my capabilities to give...

It was for me a remarkable revelation of the power of the heart to give, to love. No wonder one of the most quoted scriptures we hear is "For God so loved the world that he **gave** His only begotten Son."

The process to wholeness is a remarkable journey that not everyone will be willing to take in this life. It is filled with bumps, certain pain, and often a lot of tears. For all who seek to fulfill the plan of God in their lives or to everyone that seeks to reach their full potential, it is imperative.

There is more in you than you have seen. The diamond is there and so is the purifier of our soul, thanks be to God. He searches the deep things of our hearts; He knows the brokenness of our souls even the ones we have managed to cover over with smiles and church work or positions. No matter how loud the shouts and the glory hallelujahs they do not drown out the screaming of the inner wounded child or the yearning soul. In the stillness and quietness of the alone times, the voices roar, they thunder.

Something tells you this is not it; something tells you that there is more and that it can be yours, that God wants it to be yours and mine. Whom the Son sets free, is free indeed but there is a path to your freedom. Every path will not look the same, will not take the same twists and turns. We don't always know what we have to go through to get to our destiny. The truth be known if many of us did know we would try to get there another way or decide that that path is too painful. Sometimes God has to protect us from ourselves. He will show you the prize but not always everything the path will contain. For this release, this journey, this healing, I am and will be forever grateful.

Yet this is just the beginning. I wait to see what it will be. I hear Him calling me to another level a new position. I am admonished, "Learn quickly Janet, speed up the process, time is of the essence," I hear Him say. Whatever He places on your heart to do to get there, do not hesitate, do not delay. Turn down your plate if you must, draw away if you must, give it up, put it down, turn away, let it go. Pursue God, His best is best, and it is yours.

Thank you, Father...

Time 8:29p.m.

During my sister's visit in the summer of 2006. I remember sensing her hunger, as though she were searching for something more. Just the fact that she had taken a trip without her children, which she never did, let me know she really needed this time and that the unrest I felt for her was real. Here, she was able to exhale and be herself. I did not need anything from her. It was a time of rejuvenation, a time of honest sharing and just being.

It just so happened that our Regional Youth Encounter took place around that same time and I was eager for her to attend with me. At one of the services as we worshipped the presence of the Holy Spirit was certainly evident. I saw something happen within my sister. As she worshipped her very countenance seemed to transform. Something happened!

It was as though she came to a place of knowing. We spent many hours during that visit talking and praying, still, there were some things we did not say. I heard her heart, heard the inner wrestle and pain too. By the time she was returning to England, there was a renewed commitment with a fire and sense of purpose. She told me that she now knew what it was she needed to do.

During the next few months, it was quite evident the miraculous change this release had made in my sister's life. Soon I was receiving calls from England, close friends and members from the church we had been attending some twenty years ago, were all inquiring as to what had happened on her last visit with me to cause this transformation. She was more focused on going out, finding those who the Lord had laid on her heart, and giving them quite unapologetically exactly what God told her to. There was a new boldness and a deeper commitment to touch others for Christ, and it was noticed. It was during this time that the preceding letter had been sent the call made and we had that moment of joint release. With this release and freedom came clarity and a greater sense of urgency to walk in and complete God's divine purpose.

Each week we spoke I could hear in her voice a single-mindedness to seek and follow God's direction in her life. She was spending more and more time in prayer, seeking out those who were placed on her heart. Speaking words of encouragement, discernment, and prophetic words into the lives of others.

Dawn always had a quiet spirit of discernment and a gift of word of knowledge. It was a gift that had drawn people to her all her life. Always the protector and the caretaker she had been the anchor of the family and a dependable strength that nothing ever got to. Now she was like a quiet storm that was no longer silent. The fire was ablaze like Jeremiah, the fire in her bones could no longer be contained or hidden.

Like a man brought back from the brink of death, every moment became a precious moment not to be wasted or taken for granted. More and more she expressed that she could not sit back any longer. She admitted that she had spent the past twenty years serving her family, husband, and children, giving so much to them that there was often little left for God, herself, or to follow the path of ministry she knew God had for her to walk in.

As for me I had gone from being the baby the one she had cared for and mothered to the one who was now the caretaker. The life that we lived as children had brought us incredibly close, our spirits inseparable and connected. This time I was covering her, and it felt so strange. Yet liberating, I had my own name now. Even though I was still Dawn's little sister, I now had a voice and that voice was strong, not weak. She was looking at me with different eyes. I was aware and mindful that at this time it was she who needed me. Though we were far apart we were even closer than before. We talked every week, shared our hearts, encouraged, and laughed together.

Seven months after this initial writing began, May 15th, 2007, approximately 10 p.m. I received a call. That promised to shatter my world yet again.

It was my dear brother-in-law, he was usually upbeat and always had a wisecrack or something to make me laugh but this time his voice sounded different. I knew something was wrong and I thought that one of the children had gotten into trouble. I was not prepared to hear these words. "Bungy she's gone.... She's gone!!!!," he said with urgent tension.

I'm sure I stopped breathing for a moment frozen. A little voice began to creep in, 'See once again she's left you, if only you had been there you could have....' I almost gave in but then a sudden calm came over me. I sat down and listened. She had just slipped away. She wasn't sick, wasn't complaining of any ill feelings.

My dear sister had suddenly died, leaving a husband and four children, the youngest being ten years old. At age forty-seven years old she had finished her course and the Master had called her home to rest.

I had just spoken to her three days before her passing on Sunday, the following Tuesday, she was gone. That night after hanging up from my brother-in-law, I called my supervisor at work so they would know I had to leave. By the next day, my colleagues from the school where I worked, had pulled their resources together and made sure my flight was booked, and I would have whatever time I needed. God's provision was unmistakable.

So, I rushed home to England, wondering how on earth I would manage in this world without her. Now both women in my life were gone, both quickly both unexpectedly. How would I be able to protect her children who were now suddenly without the strong covering of their mother?

When I arrived, I found my family fragmented and understandably devastated. She had not been ill neither had there been any complaints. The moments leading to her passing were not eventful, but they were extraordinary. While watching a movie in bed with her teenage daughter she sends a text to her eldest son who was away at college, "Goodnight son, I love you and remember the Lord loves you too." Her eldest daughter steps out of the room for a moment. Within minutes of returning to continue the movie, her daughter notices she is not moving. As quick as that, no sound, no struggle she was gone.

Three weeks of autopsies and investigations found no history or evidence of any illness or anything that could explain her death. No heart attack, no stroke, no high blood pressure, or aneurism. No headache or cold, nothing that man could find. The coroner's conclusion and report read unspecified natural causes yet, strangely enough, I was at peace.

Before arriving in England, I expressed to her husband that I did not believe that the investigations would find anything. The very night I received that fateful call I saw her. I cannot say I was dreaming because I do not remember being asleep. Yet, I saw her lying there in bed, she hears God calling and her eyes are open, in that moment she is given a glimpse of the glory and the rest that is waiting there. He shows her how incredibly beautiful it all is, and He asks her if she would like to enter into His rest because he knows she is tired, and he knows she is now ready. She closes her eyes and goes home. It was beautiful; there was no struggle only sadness in leaving but a longing to go. I did not understand why I had had this vision. I could see her and feel the peace in the room, it stayed on my mind and that call made it all too clear. So, although it might have been viewed as a strange thing to say, I was convinced that the investigations would find nothing.

Once again, I found myself having to be the rock. Stepping in to get the wheels in motion and make sure we honored the memory of this great woman, mother, wife, counselor, and sister in the best possible way, a way that would make her smile and give tribute to the once hidden strengths discovered. Those that knew us were afraid for me, those that knew the God in me, must have known that my God would indeed rise up in me beyond what I would need, enough for me to be the rock, the shoulder to lean on. The one to come in and take part of the lead for all that would need to be done, I was not alone either. Of course, Russell was there. God had also given me an armor bearer like no other. Through God's providence, we had met at a job interview. I was the one seeking the job and Doreen was the interviewer. We worked together but lived vastly different lives, yet God had a plan, and I was a part of that plan to reach a heart that had called on His name. There was something about her heart and I knew that it was right where God needed me to be. Through our subsequent friendship, Doreen had given her heart to the Lord. Her hunger and commitment to serve Him were real. We were bonded through Christ. Doreen was a friend, sister, warrior. She had been there with me when my mother passed, she had been there as one of the people who had partnered with me in prayer in my time of sickness and much more. Doreen was the one that traveled with me in ministry making sure everything was in place and that I was free to focus on the ministry at hand. Here again, Doreen stood in the gap. God knew I could trust her, even with my vulnerability. She would make sure I did not crumble under the weight of being once again the wounded healer. Everyone should be fortunate enough to have someone in their corner that wants nothing but the best for them, someone sold out to the service of God and understands that those who stand in the forefront need covering too...

Tribute from a Sister's Heart's Eye

It was also my honor to perform the eulogy for my sister. It was only right, for no one knew her, knew her spirit the way I did. As I stood there defiant to every emotion inside of me that wanted to scream out. There stood Doreen, standing in position, guarding my wounded heart in the spirit. As I stood ready to speak, as I attempted out of my pain to open my mouth, my spirit brother Fitz-Arthur who had flown to England to surprise me walked through the doors of the church. Grateful tears began to well on the inside and I took a deep, deep breath. God knows who and what you need when you need it. I was not alone. Their physical presence represented God's detailed care for me.

Following her departure, in a dream, I saw my sister. She came to me and told me where in her home to find her journals. Some may say this is crazy and maybe it is. All I know is it was real for me, I felt her. She was fine, there was a peace about her. She knew I would have questions and just wanted me to understand the deeper issues that had troubled her.

When I arrived at her home I did as I was led to. I told her daughter about the visitation and together we found several journals in the very locations, she had shown me in the dream. Imagine without knowing it for years, even across continents, we were both lead to chronicle our spiritual journey, thoughts, yearnings, prayers, encounters, struggles, highs, and lows.

I now have her journals, I have her words, and I know her thoughts and struggles for all those years leading to her departure. In one of them, I found a letter of thanks that was written to me. She had never told me about it, never given it to me but it was there. It is titled, 'To my loving baby sister.' Having felt as though I only existed in her shadow I could not help myself, its contents brought tears streaming down my cheeks and a great sense of pride as it chronicled who I had been and what I meant in her life through her heart's eye. I was the strong one? The one who brought laughter in her life. I was the baby sister she couldn't imagine being without, who she wouldn't change for the world. The one whom she had painfully released because she wanted to see me soar. She loved me enough to let me go even though it had been difficult and was proud of me. Wow! Wow!

The truth was, we did not only survive, but we also overcame through the Blood of the Lamb, now she and I were completely free. It is amazing but certainly true that when a piece of you is taken you truly feel the void, you physically experience a departure in your being, and it can leave you almost breathless. I can remember one of the initial reactions to my sister's sudden departure from this world was to tell myself to keep on breathing. Take a breath I kept telling myself, come on girl breath. You feel as though you are suspended in time and for a moment the world stands still, and you have to tell yourself, you can't stop breathing you've got to keep going.

Though there were tears, I did not weep in despair. This woman, who God had given me as my sister, mentor (Mother figure), and friend, and a protective cover for so many years had poured so much into my life. I still knew though we were separated in the natural I would never be without her. There were no regrets for things left unsaid because we had especially in those last few months poured out of ourselves. God had brought newfound respect, adoration and above all Godly insight and understanding of the struggles and pain, we had both carried all those years in silence.

I could feel her every step of the way helping to get things exactly right in honoring her memory. God's grace, power, and the memory of her solid faith gave me the strength to perform her eulogy. I knew it was for me to do. How my heart ached for her children. Their covering, their glue was gone, and I prayed that there would be guidance in knowing how to minister and to reach them. As she lay there at the homegoing it would be her one last visible testimony for all who attended to witness.

Her spirit, her presence, and essence echoed throughout the building. I am at rest, we have overcome; hold fast my dear loved ones. I have loved you all with all I was able to give. I have listened to and carried many of you, pushing you to stand though my legs were weak. Poured into and fed from my very soul and spirit, even when I was hungering for the same. I have been the glue while feeling as though I may fall apart. I put you first because I have loved you as Christ had loved me. I would love to stay but I have seen my Master's face and I must take my rest. Be strong, serve Him all you can, this thing is for real, hold on and we will meet again. Even in her passing God's mercy was such that in her death it became a time of deep convicting reflection. Her impact and all she had done silently came to light as we saw the church building filled to overflowing, over 500 plus the media coverage. She had raised large sums for the local government to aid the education of low-income children. Spearheaded a project for women's needs in the community. His grace was such that because she had been set free there were those whose lives were forever changed, renewed, and rededicated.

It is one of the great mysteries, how God can bring such abundant bright life out of what is often for most, a dark time. For those of us who are believers in Christ saying goodbye is not really goodbye, but I'll see you again. For us, it is a time to celebrate life, a homegoing and not a funeral.

Today, my father is sold out to the Lord ministering full out in the Body of Christ. Who would have thought, who could have imagined? I am so very full of love and gratitude to my Savior. I am grateful for all the memories we are now making as father and daughter. God gave supernatural healing and brought a new man, a man of God sold out to the Lord and His kingdom. Hallelujah! The years of prayers and tears on behalf of our parents were not in vain. The wanting, the yearning, and desire to know that they too would come to know the joy of a surrendered life to Christ; has all come to pass. Today it blows my mind to see what God has done. It truly is no secret what God can and will do. Don't you ever stop believing, don't ever stop praying, don't stop loving and forgiving. We all fail, we all fall short God knows, yet the Father still cares. He cares enough to reach into that secret place, that dark place, that almost forgotten place, the difficult place of your hurt, your wound of the past. The broken places where those ghosts of long ago seem to lurk. He cares enough to crush the identity others give us that we so often walk in as our truth. Don't you feel the real you struggling to get out of the box others have pushed you to be self-confined to? It is so important to be elevated beyond where you are. You must believe in all God has said you can be.

Even if you don't see it yet, give Him praise. Worship despite what you see and feel, let your faith rise to see beyond your eyes. Study His word so that you will KNOW your truth. You are more than a conquer, an overcomer, a winner, you are the head and not the tail, you are not forgotten but you have been chosen. When you are in truth cry out in faith, God Himself will bow His ear to hear from heaven. He will destroy yokes and move mountains to come to see about you. When you finally get to the place where you can do no more in and of yourself, God will.

David declares in the book of 2 Samuel 22: 5-7:

> **5. When the waves of death compassed me, the flood of ungodly men made me afraid;**
>
> **6: The sorrows of hell compassed me about; the snares of death prevented me.**
>
> **7:IN MY DISTRESS I called upon the Lord and cried to my God: and he did hear my voice out of his temple, and my cry did enter into his ears.**

David's song goes on to describe how God Himself in response to the cry of His child bows the very heavens, thunders on the clouds, and comes down to save. You've not gone too far that God's love cannot find you, save you, redeem you, heal you and bring you out.

> **Verse 18: He delivered me from my strong enemy, and from him that hated me: for they were too strong for me.**
>
> **19: They prevented me in the day of my calamity: But the LORD was my stay.**

When the memories, the burden, the weight, the guilt, the struggle on this journey to not just holiness but wholeness becomes too much, and it seems as though the snares of this life are about to overtake you. In your distress cry out, refuse to be silent and suffer, don't wither, and die in your dry place. Raise your head, lift your voice and cry out to God for it is His promise, the Word declares it, He will come to see about you.

My time at home would only reveal much more unspoken words that had been bottled for years, more family pain that extended to the next generation. This was not the end of the release that was to come. It was clear to me that in my family a new journey had now begun.

Food for Thought

Just as you are moving forward, just as you finally feel as though the drama and mayhem have subsided. Something inevitably comes along that will try to take away your joy, your progress, your peace, your victory. We forget  sometimes that life is filled with deep valleys we will have to go through and mountains that often look to be unsurmountable. In these moments remember; 2 Thessalonians 3;3 (AMP)

The Lord is faithful, and he will strengthen you [setting you on a firm foundation] and will protect and guard you from the evil one.

When you stand on the firm foundation of your faith and trust in God, He will always make provision for you. No valley is too low or mountain too high. When nothing else will do, pause and you will find that His strength was always enough.

Prayer Point

Father, sometimes I think I might break and I want to scream. When I am overwhelmed, when it is too much for me, I say, "If one more thing happens," and before I end, one more thing is here. Then I see Your face, feel Your touch and I remember. You were broken so that I would not have to stay broken.

17

Chapter

A LOVE BY GOD'S DESIGN

Two years have now passed since my sister's departure. It would have been easy to leave this story at the point of release that came for us both. However, I am compelled to leave those of you reading this with a testimony to uplift your soul. Instead of sadness, tears or loss let me share with you instead a story divinely brought about out of the sadness. Even through the hurt, loss, being striped, and being broken. Out of distress, God hears our cry from heaven, He answers, He saves, He restores. God's word is true and therefore, it should not have been a surprise to me that when I least expected it, He was able to bring forth a tale of faith and love.

Our Story In His Words

All Glory be to God for the marvelous things He has done. This story starts with two people who knew each other not but shared a common love towards the Lord. I know that blind dates are somewhat uncommon in many church circles, but that is exactly how this story begins. The first time I heard her name Janet, was from a mutual friend of ours in upstate New York, who spoke to me consistently about this young lady for about five months. There were a few things that stood out to me, she loved the Lord first and foremost, her commitment to the church, her professionalism, last but not least she was said to be beautiful inside and out. I was a little skeptical and had a hard time believing that someone with these attributes could even still be out there, let alone available. Out there she was, and it seemed the Lord had kept her just for me. The Lord, He is good and His mercy endures forever.

The Introductory Call:

While on business in Iowa I decided to listen to that tugging in my heart and give her a call. Sadly, all I got on that first call was her voicemail. The message I left was not anything special, but I'm glad that God can make something out of nothing and make it a great thing.

Two hours later she called me back and we spoke briefly. We arranged to talk again a couple of days later. The second conversation would prove to be pivotal. I found her to be engaging in conversation, intelligent and I loved her voice.

We seemed to speak so easily about everything. Our thoughts were alike, we enjoyed many of the same things, travel, family, business, etc., it was as if our lives were moving on a parallel plain and all we had to do is meet.

I planned to talk with her two or three times before my visit but it turned out that we spoke almost every day. After talking to her for about a month, I thought it was time for me to place a face to the name and the voice. I decided to step up and step out in faith and ask her to meet me, there was a little conflict with her schedule but finally, she agreed, and I went to work to create an elegant evening to remember.

Our night was going to consist of a Broadway show and dinner for two, the whole evening we would have a chauffeured driven limousine. There was only one problem. I had never seen her. That is right she had refused to send any photos, so here I was all this talking and I had no idea what she looked like. Still, I had peace, I knew God was in control.

The Day of Our First Meeting:

As my plane approached New York City, I suddenly became extremely nervous as if I knew that I was about to meet my destiny, but still, there was some doubt. As our meeting drew near the driver called me to let me know that he was in position. The next call was from Janet stating she was 10 minutes away. As I sat in the lobby my first thought was to hide in a corner, just so I could get a glimpse first but then I decided to sit where I could be seen, take it all full-on, this was it. My plans were when she arrived, I would shake her hand and then escort her to the waiting limo.

Well, it didn't go as planned because as soon as I saw her, my heart was overwhelmed, all I could do was smile and move towards her. I greeted her with a hug and a kiss on the cheek. We locked hands as I lead her to the waiting limo, and I don't believe our hands released the entire night until we parted at the end of the evening. The connection was definitely undeniable.

When Sunday Came:

I did not think that I could feel any stronger for her or that this visit could be any better, but I was mistaken. The following day on Sunday, at church, I observed as another dimension of this woman became clear. Her worship, praise, and thanks unto God were freely given. I couldn't help be drawn to the visible outpouring of her inner spirit. I must admit that it took my love for her to a whole other level. The rest, as they say, is history and this was how our story began.

This walk thus far has been excellent and I look forward to whatever the Lord has in store for us both. I am blessed that God has given me another chance to love. I will love, cherish, adore and provide for her as long as I shall live. She is my soulmate, and we will be best friends, family, lovers, and partners.

Thank you, Lord, for the gift of love.

Food for Thought:

Sometimes when life throws you unexpected curves. When the normalcy of your world as you have known it is thrown upside down by heartache, grief, and loss. It can be difficult to think about, much less see where, when, or if your heart might open again. Losing a spouse or partner you have built a life with, can leave you wondering if your heart could possibly have room to love another. Will there be another that could love you. The prospect of getting back out there can be daunting and even scary. Yes, it takes time and yes you must be ready. You must be willing to be vulnerable again. God knows us better than we know ourselves. When the time is right when you feel the calling in your soul. If you will dare to put your fears aside and step out in faith, without putting pressure on yourself. It can happen unexpectedly. You may be pleasantly surprised to find out that on the other side of grief there is the possibility of love. There is room in the human heart to love again.

Prayer Point:

Lord, I am so grateful that though fear can sometimes stop us from comprehending beyond what the eyes see. Your plans for us are so much greater. How wonderful it is to know that You Lord can take us to the other side of grief and loss. And as we walk in the darkness of uncertainty, you will light the path and point the way. When we do not know how to move on from our pain, You gently cover and guide us to a place of peace. How amazing, how very precious it is to be assured that You never leave us, that You hear us. Today I give You my fears, today I accept that You oh Lord can and will help my heart to heal. On the other side of this, You are more than able to restore. I now believe that because of Your care, on the other side of grief there can still be love.

18

Chapter

OUR STORY THROUGH HER EYES:

The Beginning:

If I am asked how this story began, it would be easy for me to say it began with a phone call. In retrospect, the truth would be, way before that phone call there was a young woman who had finally journeyed to the point in her life where she was able to pray a prayer handing to God all the desires of her heart.

A wise mother in the church fondly known as Grandma Fraizer would always encourage the younger ladies with the words, "Baby, there is good, there is better, and there is best. You just hold on to God through everything life throws at you and allow him to bring you His best."

Through the years those words have certainly come back to mind many times and I believed them. I prayed just that, that I would despite the hurts of the past be open to God's best and that I would have the discernment to recognize God's best thing for me. Nothing less than a

God thing would do. Of course, like so many ladies I had moments when I wondered when He would hear me.

Especially seeing as I already had a picture in my mind of what the best for me was. Funny how we often think we can help God out. How wonderful to know that in His mercy God can look beyond our foolishness and still work in mysterious ways.

I can remember the day I received that first call, sitting in a park; I had been on a three-week fast and consecration. I had truly reached a breaking point, needing the kind of intervention and move in my life that only God could do. Each day I would disappear during my break at work. I would drive to a nearby park, read, pray and listen to a song, 'I want to Believe,' from the album, Fight For My Life (By Kirk Franklyn). If you get a chance listen to the words of that song. It ministered to me each and every time. Peeling back my every thought and prayer. I sat there in my car playing the song, singing out to the top of my voice; tears would be flowing as the words would be speaking so clearly my souls' cry. On this particular day during my break, just when I finished reading and praying in the car, I realized there was a missed call and message on my cell.

Who would have known that by taking the moment that afternoon to return that call I was stepping through a door that would lead me into God's plan for me?

After that first call, all I knew was that there was a brother, a minister from another State who was going to be visiting my area and wanted the directions to the church I happen to be attending. I was accustomed to being one of the welcoming hosts to fellow Believers that visited from out of town, so I thought nothing of it. Thinking this was one of those opportunities to minister and help someone else, I asked him if he needed help with airport transportation and assured him that I would be sure to alert the pastor and that he would be welcomed to the church, strangely enough, what I forgot to ask him at the end of that first call was how he knew my name and how did he get my number.

The details of the next month seemed so incidental, and yet they were profound and the connection that developed came suddenly, and yet it was very real. By our third conversation, I knew that there was something there. What reached out to me was that I sensed this man had a heart that was warm, sincere, and honest. Most of us ladies when we are of a certain age and experienced many of the twists and turns life can throw at us, we tend not to want to play courtship games, especially with our hearts. There was no pretense or hiding and it was refreshing. As he talked, I listened and heard his heart, or at least I felt his heart reaching out to me.

Still, a part of me wanted to keep my guard up. That's something else we ladies learn to do over the years especially if you have been hurt or disappointed in the past. Self-preservation kicks in, and yet here to my surprise the guard was not necessary. There was no sense of uneasiness, only a calm I could not explain and that made me a little leery. I wondered how it was that even though I did not know him, had not seen him, he seemed familiar and comfortable. I was beginning to look forward to his calls and sharing the day's events. However, letting him get close to me that was a different story and then I heard this word in my spirits' ear.

"You cannot keep asking me for something you are not prepared to receive. Gifts can only be received by open hands. Are your hands open?"

Well, that was a necessary blow to all the walls, guards, and locks I thought I had to keep in place. How often have you, like me, prayed that prayer, 'Lord lead me, work on my behalf, or show me your will.' Yet we struggle to follow, or move as He prompts? We forget sometimes, we don't need to know where He is taking us; we just need to know that HE is the one taking us on the journey.

Setting The Date:

Just over a month after that first conversation, we would meet for the first time. He had asked if I would accompany him to a Broadway show. It sounded enticing, but I had to let him know I was officiating a 4 p.m.

wedding that day and so it was unlikely. He didn't give up and I agreed. But not before I had shared and sort counsel from one of my spiritual fathers, who I found out had known him since he was a child. I knew before I met him that my heart had been opened to him, I was not sure what that would mean when we eventually connected, if anything at all, and that was perfectly fine with me as I didn't need to be anxious. I was sure that God was covering me and there was peace.

We talked almost every night and shared so much that as the time drew close for us to meet it didn't feel as though I would be meeting a stranger, just someone I had never seen, which I found quite humorous. Then there was the issue of how we would recognize each other. He had sent me a few photos via text, however, I had refused to return the favor, so he had no idea what I looked like.

A Meeting of Hearts

On the day we were to meet it was a very busy day. My focus was on the wedding ceremony and the couple, however, once the ceremony was complete and we had transitioned into the reception, the groom who was also a dear friend came over and with a smile said, "Sis don't YOU have something you need to get ready for."

That was my queue and all at once I must confess, I was nervous. I felt as though I was in a dream. For some reason, I knew I had to meet him and had received an okay from my spiritual dad. Which was so out of character for me still I knew I needed to go. It felt as though I was on my way to my destiny, but how could that be?

I remember walking into the lobby of the hotel he was staying at. There were three men there, but I knew him. Our eyes locked immediately, both smiling, we walked toward each other and embraced as though we were old friends reuniting. The moment I saw him I knew it was him. This man took my hand and I was speechless. The evening was beautiful, no! It was perfect in every way. Once our hands met and locked, we never let go.

I kept thinking, who is this man and where did he come from? How did he find me? I must have sat there in the limousine staring at him speechless for about forty minutes while we drove into the city. I think he started to get nervous because although we had been talking every night for almost a month I was lost for words and just kept staring.

Then, I remembered God is sovereign. He is God and He is not confined to space or time. He knows the desires of our hearts and in His time, if we just trust Him, follow after Him and seek Him, it's when you understand that He is all you need and you seek Him first and only. He will astound even the faint in heart. The rest as they say is history.

The Covering...

We were not on our own in this, but from the onset we had some key people watching out for us, specifically giving and spiritual covering. Thank you, Bishop McKinnon, for your fatherly advice, Bishop and Sister Rogers. I could always talk to you honestly. Thank you for always treating and loving me so that I could feel like one of your own. Sister Richie and my close family of spiritual brothers and sisters, June & Robert, Fitz & Delores, Virginia & Mike, Russell, Doreen.

Mom and Dad Pratt, Margarita, Marcus, Randy 3rd, Natalia, and Tamera, you are all a part of the story. Each day and for always I am covering you from my heart with my love and prayers.

Where We are Today...

Still in awe of God. It is good to know without a doubt I am just where I am meant to be. It did not come as I thought or how I thought, yet there has been a peace from the onset. More than fulfilling my desire or hearing my prayer for a God thing. God has surprised me with a love far more wonderful than I had dreamed of; He has given me His best. God has not only given me three wonderful stepchildren to love on but four astounding grandbabies to swoon over. God even went beyond that. He heard that deep longing and cry of my heart. Even though I was past the age of forty, God fortified my womb and showed to me a new incredible love in the form of our baby boy Carrington. Together we now continue to look forward, moving in God's purpose for ministry serving in the Kingdom.

Learning to love each other as an act of worship, we endeavor to honor the One who brought us together.

From My Heart...

Mr. Randolph Omelius Pratt, Jr. each day I wake, I find I love you differently than when we began this journey yet, more deeply. With you, I am stronger. I recognize your care and covering for me. I'm so very glad, the warm sincere heart I felt that first day over the phone is real. You continue to give of yourself. You found me, drew me gently, and covered my heart with your love. Thank you, baby.

Though we were on different sides of the United States, living our lives in two different worlds, God somehow knew we would one day need each other. Each day I am thankful to the One who made it all possible.

Psalm 27:14 says, Wait on the Lord, be of good courage,

and He shall strengthen thine heart;

wait, I say, on the Lord!

_____I waited!!

This is not the end of our story but merely the beginning of a glorious chapter.

Food for Thought

When you finally resign yourself to walking and looking to God only, as the one that can fill your heart and soul. You will find that all you were searching for He has. Even those things you didn't even know you wanted and needed because He is God, He has already put it all in place. And in the fullness of time, as you focus on positioning yourself where the Master leads. He will Himself astound and overwhelm you. It would be so much easier if the fullness of time came when we thought it should, but God knows us all so much better than we know ourselves. His timing is perfect, it is right, it is just. He knows the plans He has for you and me. His plans are still perfect and intended for our good. When it comes, it will be more than you had imagined. Trust Him!

Prayer Point

Father help me to be willing to wait on you. To seek you daily, to serve, and wait in patient expectation. I know that You know the longings of my soul and that You know what is best for me and when it is best for me. However, and whenever You decide to answer my heart, I will trust You. I will call out to You and I will not let my hope or faith fade into despair.

So, I look for You, I look for Your hand and I praise You in advance. I am persuaded it will be well, for whatever you decide.

19
Chapter

DADDY'S HOME

The purpose of sharing this journey is although it has been my story, each time I have counseled others or had the opportunity to share portions, I am overwhelmingly reminded that this story belongs to millions of others. Men and women from all walks of life who have had similar and harsher experiences. People who know what it is to struggle with finding a way to be released from the past. These dark clouds, or as I have come to call them, ghosts, that seem to cleverly hide lurking in the very crevices of the mind.

Those who have had to travel this kind of road soon find that true freedom, wholeness, or the ability to finally exhale does not happen by running away or pretending the past did not take place. Nor does it happen by hiding behind the blanket of salvation and the Holy Spirit.

Once again, I know there are those of you who have been taught that as Christians, "Old things are passed away and behold all things have become new." Yes, we are new in that moment of surrender to Christ and we accept His precious gift of salvation. The world looks new; we see things differently as we begin to walk within the newness of a spirit-led life. However, more people than would care to admit, have found that this does not mean that all the effects from the past and the ingrained habits, or embedded hurts will always suddenly disappear in that moment. We can naively ignore that inner cry for not only redemption but release, for not only healing and deliverance but wholeness. We do, without a doubt, have in this new life a sure source of hope and help to rise above everything that threatens to interrupt or draw us away from living in freedom the life intended for all who believe. Thank God for Jesus, we are encouraged and can rest assured that He is more than able to keep that which we commit? Give over into His hands.

(2 Timothy 1:12)

"For I know whom I have believed and am persuaded, that he is able to keep that which I have committed unto him against that day."

In other words, everything, every area of our lives we turn over to God we can be confident that He can turn it around; He will care for and protect. He can do above and beyond what we could ever think or imagine and what was meant to break you or destroy you, God will turn it around to build strength, discover insight, and open understanding into areas you would never have considered. Those places of hurt and brokenness can become your greatest points of breakthrough and transformations for his Glory. Your test will become your testimony, your fight becomes your place of flight, your shattered place where you exhale and find your 'Finally.' Praise God!

In Joel 2: 25 the Word declares, "I will restore to you the years the locusts have eaten, the cankerworm and the caterpillar, and the palmerworm."

Every broken relationship, every wasteland of disappointment or cesspool of past failures, all the why ME's; can become fertile ground for the manifestation of hope in God. Not only has He promised to restore but He is more than willing to do exceedingly and abundantly above all that we ask or think, according to the power (God's power) that worketh in us.

Nowhere did this restoration power of Gods' love, grace, and mercy ring truer than within the relationship I had experienced with my father. From the terrified child who shook at the very sound of his voice, having always been told not to trust him or for that fact, not to trust any man. To the bitter youth who intensely despised her father. After all, by then it had been ingrained in my mind that he was the cause of all the unhappiness, isolation, and turmoil in our family. There was in my being a constant grappling with the many emotional and psychological contradictions I experienced. The internal war began as early as I can remember. The constant internal battle of wanting to feel warm, loved, secure, and protected by daddy was not in harmony with the sounds that filled our home. You could tangibly feel the spiritual grey clouds of discord, hurt, brokenness, and fear. There was a constant residue from the years of arguing, tears, clashing, fighting, and then there was the deafening silence that would fill the air and choke even the thought of making a sound. Even after my mother left for the second time when

I was nine years old you could still feel it in the atmosphere. Every little girl looks to her daddy as the first hero and example of how you are loved. The thing is you do not always realize it at the time. When this is missing for whatever reason the space it leaves can become a real battleground. The distortions of what a caring relationship ought to look like, what love should feel like, or treat you were my normal. All of the basic skills for maneuvering through life's relationships, or knowing one's sense of self-worth, the lessons we are all meant to learn as children in a loving home were overshadowed by the distortions. We were silent strangers, connected it seemed only by DNA. When I became a young adult, I had moved to the States, by then we were barely cordial strangers and for years I had no idea where he was living or how to reach him.

To be honest there were many moments especially during my twenties while I seemed to be floundering around trying to figure out my direction in life, that I longed for the guidance or sound words of a daddy. In those moments God would remind me of his loving care for me throughout all those years. Yes, I had a father but when I needed it most my Heavenly Father would allow me to draw close under the shadow of His care and rest, He would cause me to experience what it was like to sit in the loving arms of a daddy. In that place, it was filled with tender touches, security, and words of assurance. I was safe.

You see when God says in His Word that He will be a friend to the friendless, mother to the motherless, or father to the fatherless He means just that.

It is sad to admit but when you have had a lifetime of being distant, hurt, or disappointed by a loved one, it's amazing how you can learn to live without ever even bothering to include them in your life anymore.

I had stayed in that place for years, ignoring the space that had been left empty, the void and secret yearning for more, for daddy. The climax of this season of my journey had taught me that these same unspoken unfelt, ignored family soul secrets, had hidden in the shadows far too long, without me even realizing it. They had wreaked havoc, fragmenting, and almost dismantling every relationship in our family...BUT GOD.

During the latter part of my sister's time here we had committed to praying for our parents. Gloriously, my mother gave her life to the Lord two years before she went home and was released from all the bitterness that had caused her so many years of unhappiness. While it is true that she may not have lived to see everything that she desired in this world, there is a tremendous solace in knowing that she found a sense of peace, rest, and a purpose far greater.

I want to pause here to encourage someone who is going through the turmoil broken family relationships can bring. Whether it is a sibling, a parent or, a spouse. You may be thinking to yourself that this has been this way for so long there is no way things are going to change. You've been hurt too many times and you don't want to be vulnerable anymore. Maybe, you have told yourself time and time again that you're fine, and you don't need them anyway. Maybe, like my story you've taught yourself not to feel in order to keep your heart protected and stay sane in an insane world. You say it is all good, yet, you know there is a longing. They are the quiet moments no one else will ever see or hear. The tears only you have been there to dry, with moments of wondering and wishing for what ifs?

Just remember there is nothing too hard for God, NOTHING! No wonder we are admonished to trust Him and not to lean on our own understanding. (Proverbs 3:5)

There is hope!

I had read this verse countless times and so many times these words of promise had given me comfort. I looked at my fragmented immediate family and hoped for the change. I have walked and outwardly seemed adjusted to the brokenness of the distant strained relationship with my father. All while still knowing the past was not erased, however, I could stand on the promise that my God would unfold a plan for a better future.

The summer of 2016 was to become a turning point and benchmark in my life. God was indeed working to not only restore but make things new. There were about two weeks left of my father's summer stay with us. Watching him light up as he and his team, consisting of his three-year-old grandson and two-year-old great-grandson tackle the garden potting and planting flowers was priceless. This man who for so much of my growing up years was scary and intimidating had become so gentle, loving, and easygoing. As we sat there overlooking the lake and enjoying each other's company I couldn't help staring at him and thinking how little I knew about the depth of this man. All the moments I had missed only made me even more grateful and mindful to cherish every second we were now able to have together. Both boys were taking their afternoon nap, instead of making myself busy in the house, I decided to sit with him and truly savor the moment. As we sat, we began to talk about general everyday things like the weather, gardening, the boys, and parenting. As we talked about parenting, it wasn't long before this became a time of sharing. The more we shared I could feel the fences of apprehension and nervousness coming down and the gates of time which had always been taboo were opening. We were both becoming individually open and vulnerable with each other. I could feel it, this was a moment that might not come again. My whole body felt as though it was getting warm. I could feel the Holy Spirit pushing me to go to that place once again.

For the first time, I was able to share with my father through the eyes of a little girl what it had been like growing up in our home. Describing the sounds, intense fear, and anxiety; notwithstanding the deep feelings of resentment. It was a difficult yet freeing experience. I tried to give him a glimpse of the emotional and psychological heaviness and distortions I had gone on to experience in my adult life.

The struggle with self-worth and the need to compromise my values or convictions to keep the peace had certainly only perpetuated my distorted view of what it was to be loved. So, I had lived too much of my adult years believing that if you don't ruffle the feathers, don't disagree, then you won't fight and he won't leave. It was okay for me to be hurt but never be the one causing the hurt.

Now please understand if I have not conveyed it, this was not a dumping session. I genuinely believe it was, however, a moment ordained for the final phase of my release or so I thought.

My father was able to share how difficult it was to come home. When he did, he observed no one in his family would say a word to him or even stay in the same room with him.

He spoke of the fights and of the fear he felt when he found himself left alone with two young girls who were indifferent to him. Not to mention a son who seemed to despise him.

He had never been allowed to, nor had he taken the time to draw close to any of us. As he spoke his head was lowered,

"I didn't know what I was supposed to do with three children. What kind of mother would leave her children, especially two young girls, and go halfway around the world when they needed her the most?" he said.

It was indeed a good question and I certainly could have come up with my own scenarios of why she would have left. The emotional, physical, and psychological abandonment. I remembered this was not the first time she had left children when overwhelmed. However, it dawned on me while he was sharing, my dad too had been wounded in this family and the toxic dysfunction of his own childhood still followed him. He seemed surprised when I noted that I had never seen them laugh, touch lovingly or say a kind word to each other. I think I wanted him to give me a different picture than the only one I had known. They had three children surely, they had love once upon a time. He thought for a moment and then confessed that it had been a struggle for such a long time he had forgotten how long. He admitted that I was probably just a baby when things seemed to fall apart.

He was hearing this for the first time, as he lifted his head, he looked at me with a look of regret and in his eyes, I knew he wished he had the right words to say. I, along with my siblings, like so many other children had been caught in the crossfire. My mother used to ask us through her tears after a fight, why didn't we come in and defend her, by speaking up and saying something? She was convinced that if we would just talk with our father, stand up to him he would change. A heavy message indeed for a seven-year-old. It had been a long and crazy journey, but here I was an adult with a family of my own and finally, I was able to rip off the last bandage and release. It had never been my fault or responsibility to fix my mother or father. They were the parents, I, my sister and brother were the children.

I must reiterate here that this was not done with any hostility. Constantly throughout our sharing, God's comfort, strength, and peace were with us, gently edging us to a place of complete transparency and healing. I had long thought of this day, it was indeed time, not just for me but for my father's healing. Some things were hard to say and others were hard to hear. Though there was a certain amount of anxiety I felt my courage and help from above. I was reminded of David the little boy with a warrior's heart. When faced with a giant it is said that David did not run but he hastened and ran towards the giant. (1Samuel 17:48). The only way to slay the giants that rise in our lives is to face them. Giants can come in all forms, self-doubt or low self-esteem, habits that seem impossible to crush whether they are physical, emotional, or psychological. Everyone faces metaphorical giants in life at one point or another.

Are you willing through Christ to face the very thing that causes you to cower or hide inside? Only then will you truly experience the awesome power of the Holy Spirit to help you destroy from the root, everything that the enemy has purposed to keep you from your promise and destiny.

At one point after a pause of silence between us, there came yet another nudge and I began to share with my father how afraid I was of him as a child. How I shook each time he called my name or if he was home and gestured for the kiss goodnight. We lived in an atmosphere of fear and uncertainty, we were always on edge. This conversation was a giant no one in our family addressed.

As we sat there his head hung down once more, his hands were clasped between his knees and I could feel the sorrow of his heart. There he was, he seemed so much larger and menacing when I was a child. I moved closer to him from across the room, reaching out I rested my hands over his clasped fingers as I sat next to him. He did not look up; he didn't need to I could feel the intensity of that moment; the walls were crumbling. I felt his heart and the sorrow of past choices. This history was indeed a part of our story. A truth we are not able to change, however, we were not destroyed nor was

I willing to let it define our lives today as father and daughter. He had carried so much inside for so long.

At that moment I gently squeezed his fingers and said, "Daddy I need you to know that I forgive you." It was not that I had any unforgiveness in my heart towards him. God had long cleansed me and renewed my love for my father. Still, I had never verbalized it to my father. I could not let the moment go by. What a pinnacle moment of release, he took a deep breath and nodded, his leg tapping and fingers wrapping around mine. I quickly realized that he had needed to hear this as much as I needed to say it to him. Time seemed to stand still in that moment as we just both kept taking those long deep breaths and silently exhaling, trying to keep control of the swelling emotions that were overflowing.

I'm not sure how long we stayed there, I do know that God was in it and it was right. God had done so much and brought us to this amazing place of peace and love. Each visit was precious as we spent time getting to know each other better. The invisible giant lurking between us had been exposed and rendered harmless and powerless. The giant's head had been cut off with the spiritual sword of God's loving forgiveness.

Praise God!

A few days later we were enjoying the presence of the Lord at a church service. The pastor delivered a powerful word on new beginnings, healing, and the need for Jesus. As the music crept towards a crescendo and the worship team permeated the air with praises, the altar began to be filled with those desiring prayer. The presence of the Lord was being manifest and the atmosphere victorious. As I stood singing with the worship team and working the altar, my eyes were brought to my father. There he was standing on the front row with the other deacons singing and carefully observing the altar. It was a beautiful sight one I became aware my mother and my sister prayed for but never got to see in this life. What a privilege God was giving me. To rewrite the later part of our family story with new memories that would be brighter than the past and give Him Glory.

My eyes kept being drawn back to my father until I saw not just a man standing there but a soul in need of covering. I felt an unction as the Holy Spirit prodded me, I got nervous and tried to ignore it. You know how we often do when we fear that we may be asked to do something a little out of our comfort zone.

That still voice whispered, you are so ready to pray with others, I want you to go over and pray, pour into your father he needs you. So right there I walked over to my father took both his hands and began to pray. The more I prayed the more the Spirit gave me to pray and the closer we came together until we were holding each other. How Glorious! More than I had imagined was melting away. My father fell sobbing into my arms, and I held him. I held him, poured into him, loved him. It kept flowing and flowing. This was it the stripping away. We had connected so deeply a few days before during our talk and poured out everything. How amazing is it that God's healing is not partial, it is complete for whoever is willing to receive it? We had emptied ourselves out and now He was using this time to pour back into our vessels. Filling us with more love and a deeper understanding. God was clearing the pathway to our hearts. This man held onto me and for the first time was receiving through me, God's touch.

This is just for you reading this right now. Your situation, your heartache is not beyond the reach of the Masters' touch. So, you think you are all alone, no one understands or cares. It's too much and it's been this way for too long. My friend, God wants you to be holy and whole, forgiven, filled, and free. Everything that the enemy meant to destroy you, God can turn it around. Job said, "Though He slay me yet will I trust him.!" (13:15). Will you trust God to lift you, to make you stronger, wiser, and more determined? He is a God of restoration and reconciliation. We may not always understand the whys of the roads He allows life to take us down. However, you must trust always that if He allows you to walk to it, He will keep you through it. It is never too late nor too far gone. He has done it for countless others and now He was doing that with me and my father.

Jesus did it and this time we could not hold back the tears. We both wept, and then wept some more. To others, it may have seemed to be too much or, maybe just a sweet father-daughter moment. Oh, but we both knew the long painful journey it had been to get to this place. This place of full restoration, healing, deliverance, and freedom.

Even now, every time I think about it, there is a warmth that flows from the inside releasing a smile from my heart that comes shining through. The cost and the losses have been great, and some have been excruciatingly painful. As a family, we had been missing from each other for such a very long time, shattered in the fragments of our own silence, hurt, and brokenness.

All I kept saying to myself as I smiled through the tears is, 'Thank you Jesus, thank you Jesus finally, finally!'

Nobody but my God could have reached so very deep into the embers of my soul, the residue of my being.

Only my Heavenly Father could have cared enough to have pierced through to the root of my soul, to rescue that little girl who for so many years was trapped hiding in the corner of that dark place. Then as only our Heavenly Father can, He chose to use that same vessel that had been wounded, broken, and marred to help bring healing, encouragement, and restoration in the lives of so many others including my sister mother, and father. You see as the potter of this vessel; God saw what I could not. When on His wheel as I bowed and began to crumble, He would gently bare me up. He did not let me crumble into a useless heap but kept spinning, kept watering, molding and reforming, squeezing and building me, from the inside out. He knew what He had put in me and what I would need to be able to hold.

You see God's miraculous work is never just about you, it extends to and through the generations of all those yet to be impacted by your life. There is a bigger picture.

The amazing awesome story here is that if you have ever found yourself wondering about the power of His love, I can tell you that there really is no greater love.

Lovingly the Word reminds us that nothing can separate us from that love. It is powerful enough to reach into the shameful places, the crevices where we tend to push those things we would rather pretend never happened. His love can reach you even when you are covered with dirt. His forgiveness is such that He will yet speak to you and call you from that dirty place. His love can rescue you from the darkest depression, any pit of self-loathing, or any prison of addiction. You can live free from the pain of shame, the guilt of sin, and the bondage of the mind. His love is more than enough to lift you from the valley of despair and place you on the mountain top of praise.

Right now, as you read, His arms of love are warmly being extended to you, waiting to lift you and carry you to a brighter place. Pause for a moment in the presence of the Holy Spirit and allow Him to minister to you.

You may say, 'But you just don't know what I've been through.' Or maybe what you've done. The bottom line is I don't know your experiences but Jesus does and yet, He still calls and extends His love to you, yes you right now! God's desires for you are still good. He says the same thing to you too. Come unto me if you are heavy laden and I will give you rest. His thoughts toward you, they are not for evil, they are for a good end. (Jeremiah 29:11) You are not reading this by accident. This is for you, or someone you know that needs to be reminded. God wants you; is concerned about you and will protect you. He wants to lift you up and set your heart dancing. He's not as far as we tell ourselves. If we could just be still, turn from the running and the hiding, we would find him right there. He is as close as your next breath. Though others may have passed you by, counted you out or, underestimated your worth, how glorious it is to know that to God you are never forgotten, never overlooked nor is there anything impossible for our God.

Your cries will not go unheard. This is not the end of your story or mine. Each day brings with it new hope new possibilities, the chance for a fresh start. Does this mean that there will never be rough days? That would be naive of me to think so. However, the peace that can be found in being transformed by His saving grace, delivered, healed, freed, and made whole cannot be shaken. Do not be trapped by your past or where you began. Your past does not have to equal your future. I know who and whose I am. Each day I am learning to live this life trusting God in, for, and through ALL things.

There are no more ghosts, no more dark spaces hidden from His light.

DADDY'S HOME! HALLELUJAH DADDY'S HOME! and it sure feels good.

Food for Thought

God can do above and beyond all we could ever think or imagine in our wildest dreams. When we pray and cry out to God, He hears more than we say, sees more than we know, and answers more than our hearts imagine. Waiting to see the manifestation in the natural of what God has already done in the spirit is often the hardest part. My friend, keep on trusting, keep believing, keep standing in your victory. In the fullness of time. At the right moment in the right season of your walk, it will come. The release, the exhale, the restoration, and the clarity. You will see what the power of His true love, forgiveness, and mercy brings, not just for you, but also for others. As you begin to walk in wholeness everyone attached to you wins.

Prayer Point

Lord, thank you for the freedom and wholeness that is found only in You. Because I am connected to others when I walk in this newness of life fully healed and whole, those connected to me can and will experience the flow of Your healing. My family can be healed, my marriage can be resurrected and my children restored. Blessing upon blessings will flow. Praise God! Your power is more than enough.

20

Chapter

LET ME ENCOURAGE YOU!

It's Never Too Late

My prayer for you in reading my story is that you have been encouraged in your own journey of faith. The journey of faith is to listen closely to God's voice calling you to a life of wholeness in Him. Maybe you have read something within these pages that resembles an element of your own journey. Maybe you are finally ready to face the ghosts hiding in your secret closet, that dark room where all the broken pieces are stored. Maybe this has helped you to better understand some of the struggles someone you know has gone or is going through. Wherever you find your thoughts going you must know God's Word is sure and His power to deliver, to heal, to free completely, and make whole is still so very real today. You may say, but so much time has gone by, does it really matter since I've learned to live with it. Or, you may say, I've prayed about it before and nothing has changed.

My friend, it is never too late for God and just because it hasn't changed yet does not mean that it will never change. So, don't wait, don't hesitate any longer.

My journey certainly was not without its own twists and turns, bumps, and moments of desperate frustration. Yet, through it all, God was guiding me to a place I had never been before. He already had in place the people who He would use to cross my path and change my life in the most profound way. To these men and women of God I encountered at Nyack College I will eternally be grateful that they did not hesitate to follow the leading of the Lord.

God himself knows that sometimes it is in the waiting, in the desert, in the dry sometimes frustrating place, we can discover His truly astounding love. It is in these places God reveals the very strength we need inside to endure, to withstand the fire, and not be consumed. God still speaks to dry bones in dry places. You don't have to be afraid of what may happen as you are going through. The three Hebrew boys did not escape the fiery furnace, God kept them in the midst of it. Not only did He keep them, but He also walked right in there with them. You are not alone even when you are on your own. When they emerged out of the fiery furnace, not even the scent of smoke was evident on them. There was no trace of anything they had gone through. You will not look like what you have been through.

Paul's journey would take him to many dark places where he could have given up or backed down. Instead, these trying times only proved to strengthen his faith. You too can refuse to die in the wilderness. Even if it seems that others have counted you out. God has promised to those who will trust Him, seek Him and follow after Him that their latter will be greater than their past.

You see your freedom and wholeness is not dependent on someone else telling you that you are worthwhile, accepting you, or honoring you. The root of your wholeness and freedom is found as you allow God himself to enter the place of your wounds to apply His cleansing blood and overflowing love. It comes as you can recognize and receive who HE says you are in Him. It is He who will transform your mourning into dancing, your tears into laughter, and sadness into joy.

Jesus has already paid the price and shed His blood for your complete healing. That includes your heart, mind, body, and soul. Your past may have condemned you, but Jesus came not to condemn you but that you might be set free and experience life abundantly.

Don't allow your fears to keep you from moving to the next level. Don't become content being up today and down tomorrow. Smiling on the outside and crying on the inside...there is more. There is a secret place, a quiet place where you can go. A place where God calls you to Himself, not so you can hide out and cower away from life but a place where He will already be there to meet with you. A place where God wants to renew, refresh transform and give you a new, more powerful walk with Him. If you are still breathing, it's not too late. You do not have to live crippled or what I like to call, 'Lopsided.'

Have you been so focused on your outward physical man that your spirit man has gone unattended, your inner voice has gone unheard? Have you been trying to live so super-spiritual that you cannot even hear the moaning of your heart, the seat of your emotional being? This season where we have found ourselves separated and, in some cases isolated, has indeed given rise to those voices. Maybe you have been able in the past to hide behind the business of your job or, all the activities and responsibilities you have carried. Like so many in this season, you have heard your voice for the first time in a long time. In this moment of stillness, you have heard the little boy, the little girl inside who had been silenced by the noise of life, screaming out, 'What about me, remember me, can I come out now? I don't want to stay forgotten. I just want to be truly free. I still hurt from the pain of the past, the secrets, they have been covered but not healed. You don't look at me, I've been hidden away, covered by your mask. You don't hear me, you don't like to acknowledge me, but in this silence, this still isolation, I rise up.'

If this is you, you do not have to hide anymore, God knows ALL about you, your past present, and future. He wants ALL of you.

His love for you is powerful in spite of, not because of.

The enemy of your soul would love for you to be dormant or not reach your full potential in God. He would love for you to keep being stumped by stinking leaking issues of the past.

He reminds you of the secret, the past, in hopes of causing you to retreat crippled into the dark shadow fearful and powerless.

BUT GOD!

God says to you today: I am here to bring to you light and life. Today it changes, today I will evict the strong man. Starting today, I give strength, power, and victory to ALL those who will be willing to move self out of the way.

Stop thinking about the other faces, or what others might say. Your journey has been different, it has been unique. If you keep trying to fit in and be like everyone else, you may never see or experience the amazing person God designed you to be.

It is, after all, those that are often seen to be scared or marred in man's eyes who are drawn and beloved by God.

His word lets us know how He feels about us. The truth is you are loved, the truth is there is power in the name of Jesus that is available to you. Instead of crumbling in condemnation from the enemy, turn the tables and tell him who he is. An accuser of the brethren, a liar, deceiver, corrupt, manipulating, defeated, destined, and doomed. Tell those whispering lies they have already lost, and that victory has come to your house.

Praise God, today you can refuse to be haunted by the past in the present. You can move into the glorious future of victory intended for you. Allow the Lord to be your king and your victory.

My friend, it is time for you to come out of the darkness into the light, to experience the love of self through the heart of the Creator. Know that God's LOVE for YOU is more powerful than you have yet experienced.

So, dare to stand up, refuse to wither away in silence any longer.

Pray for direction and help. Pray for those He will send to hold you up, hold your hand and walk beside you.

Help can come in the most unexpected places. Ask God to lead you to those who will not judge but will be willing to war in the spirit with you and pray for the discernment to be able to recognize who they are when they come.

Far too many people, far too many Christians are still suffering in the silent storm. Open your mouth, face the giant, with the one who is greater and declare like David, 'This day.'

Open the closets, set your mind and souls free from the ghosts and run. Run, fight for your life, for your wholeness, for your promise.

That's it, rise up! As you surrender into the strong arms of the Master you will finally know you were never alone, even when you felt you felt as though you were outside of His reach. It's good to be reminded that God is not thrown off nor intimidated by our dirt. We were made from dirt, He loved us and died for us while we were covered by our dirt. He loves us enough to call us and pull us completely out of that dirt.

I am praying for you, yes you, reading this right now! that you have indeed been stirred, provoked, and encouraged even while reading. I pray that today, as I have poured out of my pain and victories, you have found renewed strength to begin your journey.

One that will cause you to run with determination towards YOUR freedom and YOUR wholeness. Maybe you have been encouraged to help some else.

May God Bless and cover you. May your feet be guided in the path you should take. May your heart be strengthened, and your hope be made secure. You are a masterpiece, one of a kind uniquely designed and fully complete in Him.

Believe, do the work and you will see. The best is yet to come!

Food for thought:

Now it's all up to you, what you do with what God has stirred or provoked in your thoughts about where you are today. What has God been trying to show you? What have you been ignoring or running away from? May I remind you that God already knows. He already knows how difficult it has been, He knows about the slips and falls, He already knows the things the people or relationships that you have lost. He already sees the moments you have felt like giving up and sinking away into the dark. And you already know that what you lost had to go. When will you finally allow God to love you the way He has been waiting too? When will you dare to unlock the door? How about today, how about right now? Do you hear Him, calling you, nudging you? Please don't wait any longer, it's going to be glorious. Don't hesitate or procrastinate, it's time, it's here for YOU! and it's going to be magnificent!

Prayer Point

Lord, I hear you, I am nervous and a little afraid. Help me to not hide this time. This time I want to go all in, no holding back. I am committed to doing the work. I want to see what You will make of me. I will open my heart completely and receive ALL that You have for me. I know what You have for me is so incredibly good. I am ready to walk the path before me to wholeness, counting the cost, knowing without a doubt that this IS YOUR PERFECT WILL FOR ME!

21
Chapter

WARNING

*J*ust as editing was being completed for this book. Monday, February 22nd, 2021, around ten in the morning, I received a call that took my breath away.

My dear brother Donovan, my only brother, was found dead in his apartment. The news just did not make sense. He was the epitome of health and strength. He was an international martial arts instructor for over thirty-five years. He was a Shihan Master of Aikido. As I stood frozen listening to the news of his passing, I tried hard to stay composed, to process what this would mean, and ready myself to once again be the one who would have to be the caretaker. Once again as with my sister Dawn, I literally stopped breathing for a moment. I had to remind myself to breathe, 'come on girl breath,' I kept telling myself.

As I hung up the phone and tried to take deep breaths my mind began to race. At sixty-three years old he had never been married but did have a young son in Germany. How was I going to tell him his dad was gone? He had not seen him in person for just over a year due to covid restrictions.

Then there was my dad. His eighty-ninth birthday was approaching and I worried how he would handle the news that his only son was gone.

I had just spoken to my brother a week or two before. We talked about this book. I told him it was about to be published and to get ready because I knew some of it would be difficult for him to read and would certainly hit a chord of a time that he had not yet been ready to talk about. A time of hostility, being detached and alone. As we shared, I sensed he seemed sad, unsatisfied, and full of thoughts. At least that was just a feeling I had. For someone who had spent the last four decades traveling to some twenty-six or more countries each year, being confined and not being able to go had affected him. More than anything was the fact that he had not been able to see his son. I heard the sadness in his voice. This had been a hard year for him. We talked a little about the book, and how I had realized the need and the importance of seeking healing and wholeness from our past. He paused; we both understanding the painful place this might take him. He asked me what the title was and said he was looking forward to reading it someday. That he was proud of me for speaking out my truth, and as always sent big hugs, love, and kisses to the family.

My seven-year-old son was there when I got the call, he watched me as the tears began to roll down my cheeks. No sound, just tears, and the heavy breathing... As it hit me that both my siblings were gone now, I sat down heavily in my office chair, thoughts still racing. Then this little boy, my son, put his arms around my waist tightly, as I sat there, and just buried his head in my lap. At that moment it was everything to me. Oh, how I thanked God once again for him.

The next day my husband, my young son, and I were driving twelve hours to get to where he lived and begin the difficult process ahead.

I could not help thinking about the fact that my brother had only just begun to open the door to my father. After years of not being able to connect on any level. They had only now begun the road to mending and then healing the hurt and lingering wounds between them. 2019 was the last time they had seen each other. For the first time, they had dinner together with my brother-in-law and sat together conversing and even having polite conversation and laughter. This was now the memory my father would have to cherish. Breaking the news to my father via video call, I knew I needed someone to be with him as he was given this news.

As I told him, I saw the initial confusion the disbelief and then pain took over as he tried to find words that would not come. His only son was gone, he was not ready to be without him and I knew that. There was still too much left unfinished between them. They were just starting to come together. More than forty years had already been lost between them. I knew he was crushed. Another child is suddenly gone, no warning, no time to prepare.

It is why I decided to include this portion in my story. In the previous chapter I stated that you should not wait, don't' hesitate. My friend please take heed, look for that path and make the life-changing journey to forgiveness and wholeness.

I was reminded with my brother's passing, that it's never too late, that is, as long as you are breathing.

There is a warning here. A warning not to delay, not to remain in that dark place. It's a reminder of how important and relevant the principles in this book are.

None of us are promised tomorrow. To flourish in this life as intended we must be able to walk free from past hurts, wounds, shame, disappointments. Forgiveness is key and is often necessary if you want to be absolutely free.

My brother became a great man. I relished hearing story after story of the many ways lives all over this world were forever impacted, changed because he lived. Because he gave of himself. As I listened, at times I smiled because I knew why he did what he did for those he met. We were indeed cut from the same cloth. He had been a teacher, motivator, like an uncle, like a father to others and so much more. This was made even more evident as I experienced the overwhelming outpouring of love and respect from the martial arts community worldwide. The support was without measure. The protectiveness of those I had never known before this, let me know he was indeed loved both near and far. His whole life had become his art, his art had become his life and was his safe place.

Still, I knew he looked for peace. Did you know you can be showered with love and admiration, have accolades of greatness that hang on the walls, and yet in the stillness of just you, feel alone, cut off.

I tried to picture him in the last days of his life. What was he thinking? What was going on in his mind? Why did he seem so unsettled? As I prayed and pondered, I heard these words.

'Remind them when you speak that it is important to take time to re-evaluate your life, the relationships that you pour into, and the things you give your time to. Why do you do what you do?'

Remember you cannot become the thing you do, because when you are no longer able to do that thing, you will not know who you are. In the stillness, you will hear your inner voice crying out and not recognize it.

I wondered as I heard the words ringing if that was where my brother was. Had his identity become so wrapped up in what he did that when he was forced to sit still. When he could not travel to teach or get in the dojo to train and it was all he had done for decades, it was all he had and all he knew. Was it the reason he seemed so sad and not himself during those last few weeks of his life?

As young people in search of belonging, love, and acceptance, both I and my sister Dawn found the sense of family we longed for in the church. My brother found that sense of family in his art, to which he gave his life. Martial Arts became his world and consumed his world. We could barely keep up with his travels as he grew in rank, we saw him less and less. Before we knew it years had gone by. Still, each time we connected, he was again the protective big brother and I the baby sister. Some years ago, he began to reach out more frequently. I listened as he expressed the desire to establish some roots and not travel as much.

Just like many of you, I believe he had come to a place where he was now hearing the voice of the young boy who had kept silent about his pain all these many years. The boy who had kept running from a father he thought didn't love him. Hidden behind his work and his training were difficult memories that he had buried long ago.

He was taking stock of his life and reevaluating how he could make a change, for himself and his son. In recent days whenever we spoke, he always asked about dad, enquiring how he was doing and if dad had asked about him. I would let him know that dad was constantly asking about him and wanting to hear from him more. He would ask for dads' telephone number again, and again but not muster up the courage or make the time to call him.

My father had been patiently waiting, hoping, and looking forward to any time he could have with his son again. Dad wanted time to restore, connect and build anew. We were all proud of Donovan, respected his passion and art. But it was certainly at a cost.

Now that time dad longed for was gone. The warning and lesson here are although we tend to procrastinate, time does not. It keeps moving whether we move or not.

I could not stop my heart from going to that place of sadness for what father and son had lost, and could now never gain. What my father wanted so much to have yet did not know how to say. Neither one of them knew how to say what was in their hearts it seems. It is hard when you are a part of a family you have learned to live outside of.

When your birth family unit offers no positive sense of being, no affirmations. When there is no safe secure place of rest. When the place you grow in is cold, unstable and you are constantly on edge because you don't know what will happen next. You try not to be seen, often afraid to speak. When there is no room for your voice to be considered much less heard. There is a house but no home. You are a part of a family, but nobody is a member.

To survive you learn to live outside of that disfunction, of your family unit. There are no expectations for support from the members of the unit. You know better than to look for anyone to go out of their way for you. You learn quickly and understand that you can only count on yourself. You only have yourself. Connected forever by blood and in heart yes! Yet so very distant. This had been the experience. No parental guide or advice to lead on life's journey. So, you look for and find your sense of belonging, love, and worth outside of that place. Without the expectations, there are no disappointments. Still, there is a nagging that stays in the soul, and as you mature you realize how very much you yearn for that connectedness, love, acceptance, and security a solid family unit is meant to give. Your family was meant to give. Now both parent and child, my father and brother were trying to find their way back to a place they had never been.

To be honest it felt as though I lost my brother a long time ago, in the midst of our family brokenness. Then as a young boy, twelve years old, he discovered Aikido and it wasn't long before we would lose him to that. Nothing came before it. For the past forty-plus years, the martial arts community had become his family where he thrived and he became one of the best. But it did cost him and those that loved him. The family paid the price right along with him. Birthdays, weddings, pivotal events, even funerals he could not attend because he had to be away working his martial arts. These past few years were the best for us. Talking, laughing, listening as he shared his future plans. Just the fact we were having time was good. He had reminded me recently that he was always my big brother.

Now I was dealing with the fact that this time he would not be coming back, there would be no call, "Hi sis just checking in." No, "Tell my nephew I will get to meet and see him soon." This time we had lost him for good. I wondered did I say all I should have said, could have said, perhaps just like I knew my dad was wondering the same sentiment. Was there anything I could have done that would have not led to this place we found ourselves? The truth is it was as God our Father in heaven saw it fit to be.

You see we only have this life, right here, right now. Life is too short to live it bound by the past, caged by the pains and memories of the brokenness that lingers in our souls, trying to take control.

Healing and wholeness brings a peace that is unexplainable and sets you free to be the authentic you God originally designed you to be.

A few days after my brother's passing, as I was checking in with my dad via phone. He shared how he had been having headaches and how little he had been able to sleep which was understandable as he grappled with this unexpected loss. It was so much deeper than the physical loss of his only son, but I knew he was grieving what had been lost so many, many years ago and what he had hoped would be. There was no way that he would be able to attend the funeral service because of travel restrictions. So, I asked him what would he say to his son if he were right there, if he were standing in front of him, what would he want his son to know.

I could hear him begin to choke up, his voice sometimes staggered and trembled as he started to speak through his tears, which he was trying so hard to control.

This once invincible emotionless man, my father began to pour out his heart. My tears falling as I experienced his vulnerability and his intense inconsolable pain. I picked up a pen and wrote the words he spoke as best I could. I would have to often pause to clear the burning tears from my own eyes as I wrote. It would become a tribute to his son. His final farewell from afar.

A letter from a father's heart!

Letter From a Father's Heart:

There's so much I want to say about my son. My only son. The words are too hard to find. When he started martial arts at school, he was good at it. It was what he wanted to do, and no one could stop him. He was a white belt when he came home with a small trophy he had been given, all of twelve or thirteen years old. I was so proud but did not know how to say it. I still have that trophy with me today after all these years. He never stopped practicing and getting better. We did not see each other as often as I would have liked but he was in his way a loving son. I kept that trophy with me wherever I went, so I could have a piece of him. My love and bond to him could not be changed. He was my son. I tried writing this, but I kept crying too much to write. Even when we were apart, we were together because he was always in my heart. I love you son.

I'm sorry we couldn't be closer together over the years, to talk and laugh more, as father and son should do. You had to keep going and traveling. I would just keep asking about you and try to follow you until we could get a moment to talk. When I last saw you in 2019 that meant the world to me. To eat, talk and laugh. Son, I remember. I thought to myself looking at you...this is MY son.

I am sorry I could not be there with you now to say goodbye. My heart is broken, and it is so heavy. It has cut me to my core, and it hurts so much. We didn't get to do so much more.

I wanted to tell you how very much I loved you. We didn't get to.

> *All I know is I was doubly blessed and fortunate, beyond your death to have a son like you. Now you are gone, and I keep saying why?*
>
> *Only God knows. So, rest in peace my son.*
>
> *I love you, but God loves best.*
>
> *Dad xx*

Never had I heard my father pour out of his heart so freely to anyone ever. For over forty years he had kept my brother's first trophy, and no one even knew. I cried as I imagined how much my brother would have loved to hear these same words. He had grown, spread his wings across this globe, and helped so many others to find their way, all while desperately wishing he could find his own way home. Another wounded Healer.

We cannot change the past but we can today make changes for a brighter more vibrant tomorrow, not just for you but all those who are attached to you. I look now at his photos, I hear the stories of his greatness, his strength, selflessness, and humility and I think my dear brother if they only knew. I see you and I hear you. I understand where that strength was birthed from. Still, I also hear the silent cry that wouldn't let you stop or slow down even when you wanted to.

Again, I say to you the reader. There is still time right now for you to walk your path to wholeness. No masks no pretense. Just unapologetically free, no regrets, freely forgiven, free to forgive, fully restored.

Don't wait, don't even delay in beginning this journey toward the amazing you that God created. Don't be afraid to stop the spinning wheel and be in a still place so that you can indeed hear your own inner voices' cry.

Just take one step at a time. There's a whole cast of cheerleaders in your corner wanting you to win and to triumph. Help is available, there are better days and better days can begin today.

RESOURCES

If you are ready to begin your own journey to wholeness, and need some direction. Please feel free to reach out to one of the following professionals.

Dr. Morais L. Cassell

Ph.D., NCC, MA, MS

Behavioral Health Specialist/Therapist (ATL)

QPR Suicide Awareness (Certified)

C3 - In This Together, Director

contact@c3inthistogether.com
www.c3inthistogether.com

Dr. Roger Ball

Licensed Master Social Worker (NY)

Web: drrogerball.com

Email: drrogerball@gmail.com

Phone: 914-319-6217

Dr. Suzanne M. Howard

Certified Mental Health Coach (CT)

Pastoral Counselor, Hartford, CT, 06114,

Web: www.Suzannemhoward.com

Phone: (959) 265-0685

Pastor J. W. Pratt

(M.F.T) Marriage and Family Therapist (IL)

Conflict Resolution for Parents and Teens

Family Ministry Support Counseling

Email: Janetwa101@att.net

Phone: 708-620-4041

Lightning Source UK Ltd.
Milton Keynes UK
UKHW020808030922
408261UK00006B/132